Brunch

Great Ideas for Planning, Cooking, and Serving

Brunch

by

Pauline Durand and Yolande Languirand

Foreword by George Lang, Leading Food Consultant

BARRON'S/WOODBURY, NEW YORK

Barron's Educational Series, Inc.
113 Crossways Park Drive
Woodbury, New York 11797

© Greey de Pencier Publications Limited
59 Front Street East
Toronto, Ontario M5E 1B3

Originally published in French and copyright ©
in French by Editions Québec-Amérique

Illustrations by Jeff Wakefield

Library of Congress Cataloging in Publication Data
Durand, Pauline.
  Great ideas for planning, cooking, and serving
brunch.
  Translation of Le brunch.
  Includes index.
  1. Brunches. I. Languirand, Yolande, joint author.
II. Title
TX733.D8613   641.5'3   77-21616
ISBN 0-8120-0726-3

PRINTED IN THE UNITED STATES OF AMERICA

Contents

Foreword

From Nunchin' to Brunchin' by George Lang

Emily Post didn't write about it; unfortunately she is not around to tell me if she disapproved of it or if it simply didn't exist at the time. Webster's famed *Second International Dictionary* (1935) describes the term as "colloquial" and Elinor Ames's 1935 etiquette book says "I never liked the word *brunch* but I must admit that many hostesses feel that it describes a 'festive breakfast.'" Although it may sound like an adman's gimmicky word for a new breakfast food, everyone knows what *brunch* is nowadays. It has grown in popularity so in the past decade that it may soon become America's favorite mealtime for entertaining.

Forerunners of today's brunch were the wedding breakfast and the hunt breakfast. The first perhaps was created to satisfy the impatient bride and groom's getaway at an early time of the day instead of waiting for a late dinner party; the second developed to give strength for the huntspersons, especially since often they didn't have a chance to eat until the late afternoon. Sometimes going back too far in history makes one lose all relevance to our time. With brunch, I think the earliest comparisons we can make are with the early 16th century where, according to the Fifth Earl of Northumberland, they consumed beef, mutton, salt fish, herring, and sprats in addition to bread, ale, and wine.

In 1661 Samuel Pepys gave his friends a New Year's Day breakfast of "a barrel of oysters, a dish of meats, tongues, a dish of anchovies, wines of all sorts and Northdowne Ale." Spanish author Miguel Cervantes nicknamed the meal the "Mercy of God" because it was never refused.

One of my favorite 19th-century English volumes says that the "late breakfast" or *dejeuner à la fourchette*, which belongs to the *haute-ton* men of fashion (we were going to say men of sense), was caused because, "having no breakfast of their own, they are glad to chime in anywhere, at any hour, to get one." This early brunch was often called a "second *dejeuner*" and consisted of cold meat, reheated dishes left from the day before, some entree, omelette, bread, wine, and a pot of *confitures*.

During Victorian times both the times of meals and their contents began to change drastically. Breakfast was eaten very early in the day, between 4 and 6 AM and was nothing more than tea, bread, and butter. Dinner, which had been served in the early afternoon, became an evening affair and "nunchin" became "a piece of victual eaten between meals."

Whether Mrs. Beeton in *The Book of Household Management* (1861) created the idea of eggs in various forms for breakfast and late breakfast or if she simply recorded a prevailing custom of the day is difficult to know, but certainly her book is the first that discusses in great detail the blissful and almost inevitable polygamy of ham with eggs or bacon with eggs.

Perhaps the most exciting new flavor added to breakfast and later to brunch was chocolate (which already became popular in England toward the end of the 18th century and in the U.S. after the first factory was opened in 1765), which complemented the old standards—tea and coffee. Chocolate was considered an important potion to preserve the brilliancy of imagination or to raise the faculties of people who otherwise would be barely above the standard of a common dunce.

The Chinese never heard of the word *brunch* but they practice, especially in Canton, what in effect amounts to a brunch by serving a variety of little hot steamed and fried dumplings (*dim sum* in the south and *tien Hsin* in the north), steamed breads with various fillings, and another dozen or so special dishes that are part of this "tea lunch" meal. Although a few *dim sum* restaurants operate throughout the week in the Chinatowns of the United States and all over Hong Kong, the weekend is the time when these special treats are worked into the regular menus and whole families gather for a dazzlingly varied feast. Trays with various dishes are passed around and the diners choose what is most appealing. As the courses continue, none of the empty plates are removed from the table because the bill is computed by the waiter who counts the number of little serving plates and notes the shapes and sizes to determine the amount of the check.

"Breakfast at Brennan's" in New Orleans was probably conceived by Lucius Beebe, the man who understood the good things in life: egg dishes, marvelously complicated, oyster pan roast, honeyed breast of chicken on ham, crepes with toasted almonds, beignets with honey dip —all part of a serious brunch.

Today we can easily define the term. *Brunch* is always served on weekends and it usually takes the place of the breakfast and luncheon. Served some time between 11 AM and 3 PM, it is more than breakfast and less than a luncheon. It is an informal meal and is generally served in buffet fashion. Brunch usually consists of an alcoholic or nonalcoholic beverage, eggs in some form, perhaps some cold meat or smoked fish, and a variety of other possibilities, depending upon what part of the country in which it is being served. Fancy rolls, jam, butter, coffee, tea, and chocolate complete this elaborate collation.

But should it always be this? Should a breakfast always consist of eggs, toast, juice, and coffee? Should a dinner always be roast beef, steak, chicken, and apple pie à la mode? The pianist doesn't always play the *Minute Waltz* for an encore nor does the politician always end a speech by appealing to one's loyalty to the flag. The chef shouldn't be tied to a never-changing menu, especially at brunchtime.

By now we have arrived at the point where we can afford to create our own style, be it in decorating our apartments, choosing the clothes we wear, or deciding upon the brunch we serve. The straitjacket of the past where everything was prescribed—to the point that in my hometown in Hungary, Székesfehérvár, if you served anything but a certain type of lettuce salad with your Wiener Schnitzel, you would be locked up as a revolutionary or a lunatic—is gone. Brunch is anything you make it.

The informal nature of the meal, the time of day, and the relaxed atmosphere associated with the weekend all combine to make brunch as zany or straitlaced as the host feels.

Therefore you can have a brunch that is based on a seasonal specialty; you can have an all-seafood brunch, a vegetarian brunch, a regional brunch based on Pennsylvania Dutch, Scandinavian, or what-have-you; an icebox-cleaning brunch; a soup brunch serving several types of soups with different textures and bases; a pasta brunch with one basic pasta and four or five different sauces and garnishes; a fondue brunch or a hot pot (*shabu-shabu*) brunch; an all-*crudité* brunch; a pancake brunch using different types of fillings (meat, fish, and dessert); a *fritto misto* brunch where meat, fish, and vegetables are all batter fried; a sausage brunch or a sausage and cheese brunch; or an oyster brunch where you would serve different types of raw oysters and also oysters baked in various forms; or perhaps you would study Russian cooking and serve an interesting Russian buffet called *Zakuska*. Perhaps you might have a ham-tasting in the form of a brunch, serving different types of chutneys and fruits with the ham.

Or perhaps you can serve the original Schnitzel à la Holstein. According to carefully kept hearsay, the reigning prince of this northern German province was very fond of Wiener Schnitzel but he was also very strongly influenced by the Scandinavian neighbors and loved a variety of taste sensations featured on the great smorgasbord tables. So he ordered his chef to make the largest possible Schnitzel and when it was breaded and golden sautéd, the chef was ordered to top it with fried eggs, whole fried fresh anchovies, capers, golden-fried onion rings, ham slices, and heaven-knows-what-not. The impoverished 9th cousin of this princely gesture remains as the veal cutlet topped with fried egg, anchovy filet, capers, and a lemon slice. But perhaps using your imagination you can create the super bruncheon dish on top of a large, thin slice of Veal or Beef Paillard as homage to the prince of Holstein.

What should be your limitations in making a bruncheon menu? Only your pocketbook, your available time, and your imagination—which probably has no bounds.

Even "music to brunch by" could be part of the proceedings, since music was an inherent part of meals in the baroque era. For instance, there was a type of music that was only played in the mornings, called *Aubade*. It became a regular part of levees or receptions in the 17th and 18th centuries held by a person of high birth after rising from the bed. There is an opportunity for you tycoons with taste to commission the better composers of our day to bring back this custom, so that we can have brunch music for everyone, regardless of sex, color, nationality, age, or preference of omelette filling.

Somerset Maugham said somewhere that if you want to eat well in England you'll eat three breakfasts a day. I think soon we'll get to the point where we can paraphrase it and exchange the words *England* for *USA* and *Brunch* for *Breakfast*.

Introduction

Why brunch? First and last it makes *sense*. Alone among the odious contractions of the day— words like *mincome*, *stagflation*, *cockerpoo* and *agitprop*—it doesn't stick in the throat, and it is the only major meal, eaten in or out, that doesn't have to cost an arm and a leg.

It is essentially still a Sunday meal, served anywhere between 11 AM and 3 PM, though with the shortening work week it may soon become a Saturday fixture too. As matters stand, brunch occupies that curious Sunday period around the noon hours—hitherto a kind of ominous black hole, when the weekend papers were done with, the Sunday movies hadn't started, the wasting rigors of the night before had at last been appeased, and the rest of the day was about to be destroyed by this four-hour implosion of stupefying inertia.

Brunch started to fill that hole sometime within the last decade. Something that was neither age-old breakfast or comparatively recent lunch ("as much food," Dr. Johnson first defined it in his 1755 dictionary, "as one's hand can hold"); something instead that you could invite your friends to without the song-and-dance required by a dinner; and something you could also go out to—in the major American cities, anyway —either with your family, or with the friend you would like to make an amour, or even, perhaps, last night's amour that you would like, from now on, to be no more than a friend. In the language of the liaison, brunch makes civilized punctuation.

Naturally the type and extent of a brunch depends entirely on you and your choice of guests; but there should be one constant and that is homage to lightness.

Since the meal is part breakfast, remember eggs, bacon, sausages, good breads, jams, and coffee. Since the meal is part lunch, do not forget the possibilities of pâtés, steaming meat dishes, fritters, fish, a whole variety of salads, and even the clichéd quiche. For what room is left, bear in mind fresh fruits and cheeses: if you want to make desserts, keep them light in keeping with the intent of the meal.

The wine should be white and cool—or if you absolutely must, rosé and so cold you almost have to chip it out of the bottle. The ubiquitous Bloody Mary, complete with a stinging dash of Worcestershire sauce and a stick of celery, has become a fixture at many brunches, having ascribed to it restorative powers far in excess of reality. For those who find it unnecessarily gluttonous, the Bloody Caesar (known by many different names but basically a Bloody Mary made with clamato juice), the Bullshot (vodka and bouillon), and the Screwdriver (vodka and orange juice, ideally fresh-squeezed) or any of the other drink ideas on the following pages are able alternatives, though one should also remember that some guests will always prefer a fruit punch sans any alcohol whatever.

Most of the brunch recipes in this book are based on French cooking. Do not despair. Not all French cooking is complex and affordable only by lottery winners. These recipes are easy to prepare and—in comparison with the pleasure they'll return—for the most part, inexpensive. They ask only that you time the meal with a certain care; it's unwise to subject any meal to last-minute stresses and despite its informality, brunch is no exception. Eggs, of course, have to be prepared late in the game, and so should salads be. But many other dishes can be made well ahead of time—and you'll discover lots of these as you browse through this book.

Since this is primarily a book for the cook, we have little space for the places where you can brunch out. It's little known in smaller towns, but in the bigger cities, Sunday brunches have become a raging success. Among the popular are:

Boston

Hampshire House, Beacon Street, Boston 02108 (617) 227-9600.

Overlooking the Boston Public Garden, this building is an elegant Back Bay mansion. Dark paneled walls and paintings contribute to a romantic atmosphere. They claim they make the best Bloodies in town, and it is reported that their Eggs Benedict are superb. A tasty trout and many other dishes are good too.

Ritz-Carlton Café, Boston, 02117 (617) 536-5700.

An elegant spot, the Café at the Ritz-Carlton

offers specialties including Roast Beef Hash, Eggs Benedict, and Shirred Eggs with Chicken Livers.

Chicago

Continental Plaza's Consort Room, Chicago, 60611 (312) 943-7200.

Specialties at this high spot include a sirloin roast, chicken livers, Chicken à la King, Beef Stroganoff, roast ham and turkey, smoked salmon, tuna salad, assorted vegetables, and crêpes. Brunch is served with or without champagne.

Dallas

Brennan's of Dallas, Dallas, 75250 (214) 742-1911.

Like its New Orleans counterpart, this restaurant is well known for its Eggs Hussarde, Eggs Benedict, Eggs Sardou, calves liver, and Phannkuchen (a large crepe stuffed with chopped beef and cooked in a wine sauce).

Detroit area

Dearborn Inn, Dearborn, 48123 (313) 271-2700.

Brunch at this restaurant usually includes Chicken à la King, Eggs Benedict, a cheese omelette, pancakes, kidney stew, codfish balls, fresh fruits, and sweet rolls.

Kingsley Inn, Bloomfield Hills, 48013 (313) 644-1400.

Specialties at the Kingsley Inn include a variety of breakfast foods, juices, eggs, chicken, pancakes, Beef Stroganoff, and various fruits.

Key West

Pigeon House Patio, Key West, 33040 (305) 296-3000.

This restaurant has a daily brunch with a special champagne brunch on Sundays. It is beautifully appointed and has gourmet food. The specialties include Eggs Florentine, Eggs Lorraine, shrimp or chicken salad, and other dishes.

Santa Maria, Key West, 33040 (305) 296-5678.

At Santa Maria, bruncheon goers will find Eggs Benedict, Steak and Eggs, and a variety of omelettes in a luxurious setting.

New Haven area

Axelrod's San Francisco Emporium, Westport 06880 (203) 255-1560.

The champagne brunch includes Scrambled Eggs Nob Hill (rolled in ham and glazed with cheese), Chicken Livers with Apples and Bacon, Frisco Cristo (French Toast with Ham and Melted Cheese), and a variety of other egg dishes.

Griswold Inn, Essex, 06426 (203) 767-1812.

The Sunday Hunt Buffet at the Griswold includes the customary egg dishes plus chicken and a grits soufflé. A myriad of Currier and Ives prints line the walls; there is also a collection of firearms dating from the 15th century.

Tea and Spice, Wallingford, 06492 (203) 265-4254.

The buffet table at this establishment includes a Waldorf Salad, Spinach Salad, Eggs Benedict, Finnan Haddie, and Chicken in Wine Sauce.

New Orleans

Brennan's Restaurant, New Orleans, 70130 (504) 525-9711.

Breakfast at Brennan's is a New Orleans tradition. Try this restaurant's famous Eggs Hussarde, Eggs Sardou, and the other poached egg dishes.

Commander's Palace, New Orleans, 70130 (504) 899-8221.

Here you will find the Jazz Brunch, served every Saturday and Sunday, to the accompaniment of very fine jazz. Specialties include a Milk Punch, Eggs Hussarde, Oyster and Artichoke Crêpe, Eggs Commander's, plus Lemon Crêpe and Praline Parfait.

The Pontchartrain Hotel, New Orleans, 70140 (504) 524-0581.

In the Caribbean Room, the brunch specialties include Veal Grillades à la Creole, Chicken Hash and Grits Soufflé, and Broiled Quail. Also to be found are Hot Ginger Bread, Pot de Creme au Chocolat, and, the New Orleans favorite, Café Brulot.

New York City

Cafe des Artistes, New York, 10023 (212) 877-3500.

This continental restaurant offers such specialties as a hot Lyonnaise Sausage en Croute, Herring Filets in Apple Cream, Clams in Mignonette Sauce, and a charcuterie platter.

Windows on the World, New York, 10048 (212) 938-1111.

The dining room of this restaurant offers probably the best view of the city. The all-day buffet includes salads, roasts, charcuterie, pickled shrimp, apple-smoked chicken, and other unusual offerings.

Rainbow Room, New York, 10020 (212) 757-8970.

One of the city's most crowded brunch spots, the Rainbow Room features a fabulous view and a sampling of dishes, including smoked whitefish, duck pâté, omelettes, and fresh fruit.

San Francisco area

Davre's, San Francisco, 94104 (415) 433-7500.

The Carnelian Room features a Sunday brunch with specialties such as assorted Pacific seafood treasures, soups, a variety of omelettes, crêpes, and fresh fruits.

Rolf's, San Francisco, 94107 (415) 673-8881.

This restaurant offers a Sunday brunch that includes Eggs Benedict, French pancakes with fresh strawberries, English Bacon, and a freshly baked orange marmalade Danish.

"What's in a name?"

The origins of a classic french dish

How do dishes originate? How do they get their names? We really have no record as to when some dishes were first made, or how and why they have the names they have, but the whole realm of gastronomical history is an intriguing, never-ending topic.

Some names are given for obvious reasons —the ingredients used, the origins of the raw materials, a reference to region or origin, the manner of preparation. Something *lyonnaise* will have onion in it; anything *crécy* will have carrots; *DuBarry* (the courtesan of Louis XV) in the name will mean that the dish will include cauliflower. Argenteuil, a small French town noted for its asparagus cultivation, gives its name to dishes with that vegetable.

George Lang, a distinguished chef–restaurateur and noted international food consultant, has traced the origins of one of his favorite dishes—Pot-au-Feu. How did it originate? What are its traditional ingredients? The recipe is included in the next chapter but Mr. Lang's story of his discoveries follows.

*Pot-au-Feu: The Perfect Bruncheon Dish by George Lang

To play a game of tagline, the 18th and 19th centuries could be called the Age of Romantic Free-

*The recipe for Pot-au-Feu can be found on page 38.

dom and the 20th Century, particularly the last two decades, the age that longed for authenticity and purity.

Because of this, we freely throw words around, like *classic*, *real*, *authentic*, but when we try carefully to explore the hallowed cathedral of the past, we find that more often than not it is a labyrinth of caves often unconnected to each other. The more one probes these areas the more confusing the pattern gets.

In search of the Truth, I made it my business to refresh my knowledge about Le Pot-au-Feu. Perhaps the subtitle of this story could have been "Twenty Characters in Search of a Pot-au-Feu."

I felt there was no point going further back than Carême. His analysis and description are heavily larded with pseudo-scientific explanations (perhaps more the crime of his age than his own fault). The peculiar thing is that via Dumas, almost everybody copied these silly descriptions of the *osmazome* and other gobbledygook. That is until Elizabeth David came along and started afresh. However, Carême did lay down the basic principles of the Pot-au-Feu, namely: very, very slow, even boiling. "Haven't I seen, in our great culinary banquets given at the Hotel-de-Ville de Paris at the time of the Empire and the restoration, at the Ecole Militaire, and in the Imperial and Royal households of the Capital, where Laguipierre, Robert, Lasnes, Boucheseche, Daniel, Richard, Savard, Chaud, and Bardet were the chefs in charge; haven't I, I repeat, thousands of times heard these great masters recommend to the men in charge of putting the marmites on the fire to make them come to a 'frothing' point slowly, with a moderate fire, adding at intervals a little cool water, in order to expand the albumine which will then rise in an abundant foam. In this way, we obtain bouillon 'as good as the housewife's.'" He also discussed the necessity of using the freshest vegetables; the fact that the larger the beef cut is, the better the broth will be; and the great variety of possibilities open to the professional cook. He also opens the door to the next two hundred years' confusion by discussing the inclusion of chicken and other birds and meats.

According to strict etymology, *potée* is anything that is cooked in an earthenware casserole. The Pot-au-Feu was cooked for many years in France in an earthenware vessel that was continuously replenished (another fallacy that is demolished by Elizabeth David) and hence the name. The second fact we know is that beef is always part of this and more often than not these are the choices:

Pointe de Culotte	Sirloin Tip, Knuckle
Gîte à la Noix	Bottom Round
Paleron	Chuck Pot Roast
Mileau de Poitrine	Brisket
Jarret	(for taste only)

From here on it is stormy sailing because no two chefs agree on the rest of the ingredients or methods. Let me give you a few for instances:

A majority put in a special chicken that is ideal for boiling, some with a pork stuffing, some without. (Henry IV's P.R. pitch seems to be the same). Some include sausage, others would not think of it. Everybody puts in marrow bones, but several chefs consider it not suitable to eat for health reasons. Some chefs add pork (in some of the older cookbooks they even cook it together, horrible dictu), veal, duck, turkey, and, in the provinces, they add mutton.

In *Languedoc* it is virtually a liquid cassoulet with bacon, stuffed cabbage, and, of course, the white beans. The famous *Albigeoise* version is based on stuffed goose neck, beef, mutton, salt, raw ham, dried sausage, and preserved goose. Escoffier in his *Ma Cuisine* spends five pages on it and I must say is probably the most sensible of them all. One of the interesting variations he mentions is the Pot-au-Feu, which is served with toasted French bread, placed in alternating layers with gruyère and parmesan cheese in the serving tureen. Poached eggs are placed on the top and then the broth is poured over all. Tongue and calf's head are not used in France; this is a *Bollito Misto* specialty.

There is general agreement on the vegetables, and it is interesting to note that the clove stuck in the onion persists in each recipe from Carême on. A rather peculiar touch in this area is the version of the generally admirable Julia Child, where she puts in grilled tomato—which I think would produce a much too sour effect.

One of the vegetables that causes violent arguments among Pot-au-Feu aficionados, is the cabbage. Escoffier says, "You may leave it out." I feel that it ruins the taste, particularly if cooked in the same broth, yet I still like to serve it every now and then with boiled potatoes, which is another controversial point.

The next subject of controversy is farinaceous garniture. The majority simply mention that you can put in any kind of noodles, macaroni, or rice; some don't mention this addition at all. I personally feel that a good home-made egg noodle, particularly small in size, instead of the longer threads, would be a delightful addition to a Poule-au-Pot but not for the Pot-au-Feu. (Julia Child, by the way, suggests Risotto or buttered noodles).

An interesting variation on the essential theme is a *Zürcher Ratsherrentopf*, which is essentially a Pot-au-Feu made with veal and pork: boneless veal shoulder and pork shoulder cut into small cubes and layer by layer placed together with shredded cabbage, sliced bacon, sliced white turnip, cubes of potatoes, and chopped onion in a heavy dutch oven. It is sprinkled with salt and black pepper and cooked on top of the range or in the oven with chicken broth, until meat and vegetables are tender and the liquid is reduced by half.

To me, one of the most interesting experiences is having one basic texture and taste played against others. It is like playing with color. For instance, the same blue will look totally different against a green or a brown. According to cautious purists, the only accompaniments one should serve are the coarse salt, cornichons, mustard, and horseradish. Yet even Escoffier mentions the possibility of a tomato sauce, piquant sauce, or a horseradish sauce. Montaigne simply says, serve whatever goes well with it. Several recipes mentioned a German-type cream sauce or an Italian-style *sauce verte*, which appears even in Dubois's cookbook.

You may also add *Sauce Alsacienne*, which is very similar to a *Sauce Gribiche* (see *Le Répertoire de la Cuisine*, Barron's, 1976) or an old-fashioned sauce of reduced heavy cream simmered with prepared mustard and *concassé* of tomatoes.

There was a famed restaurant, Meissl and Schadn's in Vienna, which had 24 varieties of boiled beef on its menu. The guests knew the exact characteristics of the various cuts for boiling and it was considered as much of an exact science as sauces are in France. Each habitué had a special cut or even subcut of his or her own and would take nothing else. Luncheon was a ritual, even as to how each guest had his or her own geometric pattern of placing the vegetable on the plate. Viennese chefs never put beef into cold water if they wanted an especially succulent piece of tender beef. It was always started in boiling water, which closed the pores of the meat and kept the juices inside. If, however, they wanted an especially good broth they did start—like their French colleagues—in cold water.

As far as the accompaniments are concerned, the Viennese served some or all of the following: grated horseradish prepared either with vinegar, apple sauce, ground blanched almonds, or whipped cream; chive sauce; gherkin sauce; or anchovy sauce. There would generally be one hot sauce served, either a dill sauce, a fresh cucumber sauce, a bread sauce with horseradish, a tomato suace made with fresh, peeled tomatoes, mushroom sauce, onion sauce, or a hot almond sauce. Often salads were served with the boiled beef, mostly beets or pickles. Sauté potatoes could be part of this kingly or "Imperial" profusion. The wildest is the otherwise excellent recipe of R. A. deGroot, who suggests—among other things—whipped fresh fruits as an accompaniment.

The following story will warn you about a key point in your successful Weekend Brunch: Prince Condé was visiting the Bishop of Passau. The Bishop mentioned that he had commanded the chefs to take the greatest care in the preparation of soups because the French are a nation of soup lovers. The Prince replied, "That is true, Sire, but please remind them that the French not only love soup, but love it only boiling hot."

What should you serve with your Pot-au-Feu and in what order should it be served? As a difficult-to-do—but worth reaching for—guide, read a luncheon I prepared for the Chevaliers du Tastevin on March 9, 1968, the first lunch, to my knowledge, ever prepared for this noble organization.

RECEPTION

Chablis Grand Cru
Valmour Pic 1964

Oysters and Clams of North America
-Served From Two Silver Wagons-
Halved, Pitted Lemons and Sauce Mignonette
(To Be Served during the Exchange of
Vital Gossip)

*

IN THE DINING ROOM

Marrow in Its Own Boat Cut From Shin Bone
Pulled and Toasted Bread

The Consommé

The Beef

Corton Close des
Cortons Faiveley,
Jeroboam 1949

(Carved in the Dining Room)
Pointe de Culotte; Tranche Grasse;
Gîte à la Noix Paleron;
Milieu de Poitrine; Sirloin Tip, Knuckle
Bottom Round; Chuck Pot Roast; Brisket
Queue de Boeuf Farcie; Jarret

The Fowl Bird
(All Carved in Dining Room)
Coarse Salt, Cornichons, Moutarde Forte,
Sauce Raifort

Whole Vegetables Including:
Carrots, Leeks, Parsnips, Onions, Steamed
Potatoes

*

Krug Private Cuvee
Brut N/V

Fresh Grapefruit Sherbet
With Grapefruit Segments Served
in Their Shell
Mignardises

Cafe Noir

CONFRERIE DES CHEVALIERS DU
TASTEVIN
LUNCHEON
Saturday, March 9, 1968

Guest menus

Breakfast at Brennan's

The following is Brennan's most famous brunch, called a "Typical New Orleans Breakfast." It consists of a baked apple with double cream, Eggs Hussarde, Bananas Foster for dessert, and, of course, the meal is served with hot French bread and chicory coffee.

Eggs Hussarde

2 thin slices Canadian Bacon, grilled
2 Holland Rusks
1/4 cup Marchand de Vin sauce
1 grilled tomato
2 poached eggs
1/4 cup hollandaise sauce

On a dinner plate, lay slices of Canadian Bacon on 2 Holland Rusks, then cover each with Marchand de Vin sauce. Top now each rusk with a poached egg and cover with the hollandaise sauce. Garnish with grilled tomato. For eye appeal, you may sprinkle paprika and chopped parsley on eggs.

Marchand de Vin Sauce

3/4 cup butter
3/4 cup finely chopped mushrooms
1/2 cup minced ham
1/3 cup finely chopped shallots
1/2 cup finely chopped onions
2 tablespoons minced garlic
2 tablespoons flour
1 teaspoon salt
1 teaspoon white pepper
1/2 teaspoon Cayenne
3/4 cup beef stock
1/2 cup red wine

Melt butter in a medium-sized sauce pan and lightly sauté mushrooms, ham, shallots, onions, and garlic. When onion is golden brown, add the flour, salt, pepper, and Cayenne, then brown well, about 7-10 minutes. Blend in the stock and wine and simmer over low heat for 35 minutes.

Hollandaise Sauce

4 egg yolks
2 tablespoons lemon juice
1/2 lb. melted butter
1/4 teaspoon salt

In the top half of a double boiler, heat egg yolks and lemon juice. Cook very slowly in the double boiler over low heat, never allowing the water in the bottom pan to come to a boil. Add butter, a little at a time, stirring constantly with a wooden spoon. When mixture thickens, add salt and pepper to taste.

Bananas Foster

1/2 cup brown sugar
1 tablespoon butter
Dash of cinnamon
1 ounce banana liqueur
1 ripe banana
1 ounce rum
vanilla ice cream

Melt sugar, butter, and cinnamon in flat chafing dish; add the banana liqueur. Place the banana in the mixture and cook till tender. Flame with rum, then spoon the banana and sauce over the vanilla ice cream.

A Summer Brunch with a Mediterranean Spirit

The following menu by Paula Wolfert reflects the diversity of foods enjoyed in the regions around the Mediterranean Sea. This brunch serves 6 persons and includes an Italian omelette with artichokes, Greek cheese triangles with dill, Middle Eastern meatballs on skewers, North African carrot salad, and melon balls with anisette in the Spanish manner.

Italian Omelette with Artichokes

9 or 10 oz. package frozen artichoke hearts
1 lemon
Flour seasoned with salt and pepper
6 large eggs
3/4 teaspoon salt
1/4 teaspoon freshly ground black pepper
1/4 cup milk
1/4 cup Italian olive oil
Chopped parsley

Thaw the artichoke hearts and pat dry with paper towels. Sprinkle with lemon juice and then dust with seasoned flour.

Beat the eggs with a whisk until frothy. Season. Stir in the milk. Preheat the oven to 400°F.

Brown the artichoke hearts in hot olive oil in an 8-inch ovenproof skillet. When golden brown on all sides, pour the eggs over them. Cook over medium heat until the eggs are set on the bottom. Set the skillet in the oven and bake for 10 minutes.

Remove from the oven and allow to rest 2-3 minutes. Loosen around the edges and bottom with a spatula and turn out onto a warm serving dish. Serve warm cut in wedges.

Greek Cheese Triangles (with Dill or Fresh Marjoram)

4 oz. feta cheese; rinsed, crumbled, and pushed
   through a food mill
3 oz. creamed cottage cheese, drained
2 eggs
1-1/2 tablespoons finely snipped dill or
   crumbled marjoram
1/4 lb. filo pastry leaves (about 6 sheets)
5 tablespoons melted butter

In a mixing bowl combine the cheese; mixing
well. Add the eggs then the herbs and blend
thoroughly.

Spread a pastry leaf in front of you, keeping
the other leaves under a damp towel. Cut ver-
tically into three equal parts. Brush the surface
with melted butter. Fold each pastry leaf in
three lengthwise. Place a spoonful of filling on
each piece, one inch from the bottom. Fold the
left-hand corner over the filling so as to make
a triangle. Fold the triangle straight up, then
fold upward to the left and continue folding as
you would a flag until you reach the end and
have a neat triangle. Tuck in any loose ends and
brush with melted butter. Lightly cover and
keep in the refrigerator until you are ready to
bake.

Preheat oven to 375°F. Bake the triangles about
25 minutes or until puffy and golden brown.
Serve warm.

Skewered Meatballs in Pita Bread

1-1/2 lbs. ground beef
1 small onion, grated
3 tablespoons chopped parsley
1/2 teaspoon ground cumin
1/4 teaspoon paprika
Salt
Cayenne pepper to taste
12 small pita loaves
12 8-inch bamboo skewers

Combine all the ingredients and knead well. Let ripen at least 1 hour. With wet hands, form into 1-inch balls and pack them around 8-inch bamboo skewers, four to each one.

Grill rapidly on both sides, 2-3 inches from a broiler flame or over charcoal until done to taste. Serve, hot, at once, with pita.

Moroccan Carrot Salad

1 pound carrots
1 clove garlic
Pinch ground cinnamon
1/2 teaspoon ground cumin
1/2 teaspoon sweet paprika
Pinch of Cayenne and sugar
2-3 tablespoons lemon juice
Olive oil
Salt
2 tablespoons chopped parsley

Wash and peel carrots. Boil whole in water with the garlic until barely tender. Drain. Discard the garlic and dice or slice the carrots.

Combine the spices with the lemon juice, sugar, and salt and pour over the carrots. Chill overnight.

Sprinkle with oil and chopped parsley just before serving.

Melon Balls with Anisette

2 ripe cantaloupe
1/2 tablespoon anisette
1-1/2 tablespoons confectioners' sugar
3 tablespoons water

Halve the melon and remove the seeds. Scoop out the melon flesh in balls and place in a glass serving dish.

Combine remaining ingredients and pour over melon balls. Allow to stand in a cool place about 1 hour before serving.

Pot-au-Feu* by George Lang

In the Austro-Hungarian Empire, Vienna's fabulous boiled beef was a way of life. According to my friend Joseph Wechsberg, almost everybody followed Franz Josef's example by eating a glorious broth with beef and vegetables for luncheon virtually every day except—ironically—Sunday. At precisely 12 noon, all the church bells rang out in memory of the victory over the Turks in Constantinople many hundreds of years before, which triggered the closing of all the stores in my hometown and, since everybody lived within walking distance of their homes, within 15 minutes the aroma of this glorious pot of broth gently covered the town.*

The recipe that follows is a simplified, but certainly not bastardized, version of this dish. I made it for ten people because this dish is perfect for a party brunch and, besides that, the larger the quantity (up to a point), the better it seems to get.

I suggest that you serve at least the little cornichon pickles, freshly grated horseradish, coarse salt, and pepper freshly ground, but you may also prepare a tomato sauce or a cream horseradish sauce, or any number of other garnishes with it.

---

*Be sure to read Mr. Lang's account of his search for the origins of this dish; see pages 19-25.

Pot-au-Feu

14 lbs. short ribs of beef
2 large carrots, scraped and left whole
1/2 bunch celery, chopped
2 large onions, cut lengthwise and burned on
surface
Handful of leek trimmings
Bouquet garni—a cheesecloth bag with 2 bay
leaves, 1/2 teaspoon crumbled thyme leaves,
1 teaspoon lightly crushed peppercorns, 4
cloves, small bunch of parsley stems
1 tablespoon salt
2 teaspoons Accent
2 tablespoons chicken stock or a few chicken
bouillon cubes

Place the meat in a deep soup pot. Cover with
cold water. Bring to the boil. Simmer 15 minutes, skimming frequently. Add the carrots, celery, onions, leek trimmings, and bouquet garni
and season with salt and Accent. Lower the
heat and cook at the simmer 21/2-3 hours or
until the meat is tender, skimming frequently.
Midway add the chicken stock.

Remove ribs from cooking liquid and cut away
bones and fat. Cut in 2 crosswise.

To serve one portion, place 2 pieces of meat
in a good-sized soup plate, add 1/2 cooked leek,
a carrot, and a boiled potato. Ladle over enough
cooking liquid to cover. Serve with a small dish
of horseradish sauce, coarse salt, and gherkins.

Vegetable Accompaniments

5 parboiled leeks, halved
10 carrots, scraped, left whole and cooked until
  just tender
10 peeled and boiled potatoes, whole

A half hour before meat is done, remove several cups of broth and cook vegetables in a heavy pot with a close-fitting lid.

Horseradish Cream Sauce

1 horseradish, peeled and grated
2 cups cooking liquid
2/3 cup heavy cream
Salt, pepper, and a teaspoon of sugar
About 1/4 cup roux

Heat cooking liquid in small saucepan. Whisk in enough roux to thicken. Stir in 3/4 of the horseradish and taste. Add more if needed. Season with salt, pepper, and sugar. Simmer 10 minutes. Add the cream and simmer 5 minutes longer. This recipe makes about 2 1/2 cups.

Additional Suggestions

Get from the butcher a few pounds of beef marrow bones cut to short pieces and gently cracked by very same butcher. Tie them up in cheesecloth and cook them together with beef.

Serve scooped out marrow on a piece of roughcut crisp toast, sprinkled with coarse salt (and possibly with a touch of Cayenne pepper) either as a preliminary to the proceedings or to accompany the broth.

A much more ambitious undertaking is to turn a Pot-au-Feu brunch into a *Bollito Misto* Sunday Italian dinner. This "mixed boiled" meat feast relates to many nations' similar preparations, including the New England boiled dinner. The idea is this: you take, in addition to the beef, a whole tongue, a large poulet, Italian style cotechino or zampino sausage, or perhaps a French style Lyonnaise sausage. Cook everything in the broth. It is important to put each ingredient in at different times to make sure that nothing is overcooked.

A *Salsa Verde* or Green Herb Sauce—consisting of finely chopped or sieved hard boiled eggs, chopped anchovy filets, capers, lots of curly and flat parsley, ground or chopped spinach, garlic, bread crumbs, vinegar, salt, whipped into olive oil to a semi-liquid consistency—may be served at room temperature, as a side accompaniment.

At a large carving table or sideboard, you display all the cooked mixed meats and carve a piece for everyone, according to their liking. Whole vegetables from the broth are added on the same plate or separately, moistened with a bit of broth.

The green sauce is either served separately or put on top of the meat. You should have coarse salt, little cornichon gherkins, and strong mustard on the table.

Selected menus

The following is an assortment of menu ideas for different kinds of brunch meals. Try these menus, all of which use recipes that have been included in this book.

Champagne Buffet Brunch

Aperitif: Champagne and orange juice

Fruit: Rummy cantaloupe

Bread: Brioche endimanchée

Eggs: Lobster omelette

Meat: Stuffed ham

Pâté: Hard-cooked egg pâté

Fish: Squid with tomatoes

Cheese Tray

Salad: Endives with beets

Dessert: Tropical cream

Preparation hints:

- Garnish the cantaloupes with grapes
- Decorate the lobster omelette with watercress
- Arrange the hard-cooked egg pâté on lettuce leaves surrounded with pickles
- Cut the first slice from the stuffed ham and garnish the plate with orange slices and parsley
- Serve squid with tomatoes in a colorful bowl
- Arrange the endive and beet salad in the shape of a flower, with the beets in the center.

"I am more than happy to be able to give to my readers a piece of good news, namely that good cheer is far from being harmful to health, and that, all things being equal, gourmands live longer than other men" — Jean-Anthelme Brillat-Savarin — "La Physiologie du gout" 1825

Collective Brunch

"Fowls are to the kitchen what his canvas is to the painter." — Brillat-Savarin.

Aperitif: Rum punch

Fruit: Tipsy orange salad

Bread: Cheese bread

Eggs: Onion pie

Meat: Chicken in white wine

Fish: Fish fillets on toast

Pâté: Cognac and sherry pâté

Vegetables: Eggplant with noodles

Cheese tray

Salad: Rainbow salad

Dessert: Fruit tray

Informality is the keynote. Most of the items on this menu can be made ahead of time and brought to the party by a few of the guests.

A Prepare-Ahead Brunch

Aperitif: Bloody Mary

Fruit: Juicy peaches

Eggs: Eggs in red wine

Meat: Roast pork with pineapples

Fish: Haddock fritters

Pâté: Calves liver pâté

Vegetables: Scalloped potatoes

Salad: Green bean salad

Dessert: Coeur à la Crème

Pineapples are at their best from March through June. Select firm, heavy ones with a strong sweet pineapple aroma. The centre spikes should separate and pull apart easily.

The fritter batter, the roast pork, the pâté, the peaches, the scalloped potatoes, the Coeur à la Crème and the green bean salad can be prepared the night before and refrigerated.

On the morning of the brunch, all that is left to do is to prepare the Bloody Marys, the eggs in red wine, deep fry the fritters and make the coffee.

Budget Brunch

Grapefruit are at their best from January to May. Avoid the large puffy ones and select those which are heavy for their size. Do not be deterred by a greenish tinge which is a sign of maturity and sweetness.

Aperitif: Port Flip

Fruit: Baked grapefruit

Bread: Muffins

Eggs: Omelettes with croutons

Meat: Corned beef with pickle sauce

Fish: Tuna loaf

Vegetables: Stuffed baked tomatoes

Salad: Grated carrots with cream

This brunch for four can be made for approximately $13. Even with a couple of bottles of wine you should have some change left from $20.

Special Family Brunch

Aperitif: Screwdrivers or orange juice

Fruit: Juicy peaches

Eggs: Eggs Provençal

Meat: French meat loaf

Fish: Fish with pasta shells

Pâté: Liver pâté

Salad: Green salad vinaigrette

Dessert: Apple and pear upside-down cake

Preparation Hints:
- The pâté and meat loaf can be made a day in advance
- Several hours before the brunch, members of the family can be assigned preparation of the upside-down cake, the cooking of the peaches, and the pasta shells for the fish and pasta dish, the eggs Provençal, the making of the salad, the coffee and aperitifs.
- Just before sitting down to eat the peaches, whoever's in charge of eggs breaks them into the Provençal sauce. Someone else removes the upside-down cake from the oven, lowers the heat and puts the fish and pasta dish in to warm.
- A basket of French bread can be placed on the table with the pâté.

Brunch for Two

Aperitif: Brandy eggnog

Fruit: Baked grapefruit

Eggs: Eggs au gratin

Meat: Bacon, English style

Salad: Green peppers meridional

Dessert: Apple fritters

Four hands are needed to get all the dishes on this menu ready for serving at the same time. While one person prepares the grapefruit, the other gets the eggs au gratin ready. While one takes care of the apple fritters, the other can be cooking the bacon, mixing the aperitifs and setting the table. The peppers can be prepared the evening before.

Serve with any breads.

Campfire Brunch

Aperitif: Red eye

Fruit: Tipsy orange salad

Eggs: Stuffed hard-cooked eggs

Meat: Pork and beans with beer

Vegetable: Potato pancake

Salad: Dandelion salad

"Always remember that I have taken more out of alcohol than alcohol has taken out of me."
— Sir Winston Churchill

Half the fun of this meal is waking up in camp to the tantalizing aroma of pork and beans that have been on the fire all night. Soak the beans for a couple of days. Then the night before your brunch build an enormous campfire on some sand. When the flames have died down cover the bean pot with aluminum foil and place it in the hot sand. Cover with coals.

Après-Ski Brunch

Aperitif: Caribou

Fruit: Grilled grapefruit

Bread: Muffins

Eggs: Quiche Lorraine

Meat: Spiced sausage and potato stew

Fish: Grilled smelts

Pâté: Head cheese

Vegetable: Kidney beans in red wine

Salad: Green salad vinaigrette

Dessert: Dried fruit compote

This hearty feast is really delightful after an early morning ski. The Caribou, a potent drink, is made as follows:

Caribou

1 bottle of Loganberry wine

10 ounces 80 proof Alcohol (40 A/V)

Mix well. Serve with or without ice. Serves four.

Hunting Brunch

Aperitif: Red eye

Fruit: Fruit plate

Eggs: Omelette with croûtons

Meat: Pork and beans with beer and home-
   style ketchup

Fish: Squid with tomato and red pepper

Pâte: Liver pâté

Salad: Prunes in red wine

Dessert: Raspberry or apple mousse

The beans and pâté should be prepared the day
before. The squid must marinate overnight, and
the prunes are best if cooked two or even three
days ahead.

   If you are slicing the fruit, sprinkle the pieces
with lemon juice so that they don't discolor.
Have the croûtons ready so that the omelette
can be served immediately. Whip the mousse
when your guests are ready for dessert. It takes
only moments to prepare and must be served
right away.

Skating Brunch

Aperitif: Hot gin: 2 oz. hot dry gin
   6 oz. hot water 1 teaspoon honey or sugar
Fruit: Compote of dried fruits
Eggs: Cheese and ham soufflé
Meat: Spiced sausage and potato stew
Fish: Grilled smelts
Bread: Muffins
Cheese Tray
Salad: Green bean salad
Dessert: Apple Beignets (fritters)

The compote, stew, and green bean salad can be prepared the day before. Salt the smelts and pre-heat the broiler half an hour before grilling. The soufflé eggs should be room temperature or should sit for 20 minutes in a bowl of warm water.

One hour before serving time, arrange the cheese tray so that the cheese can ripen. The fritter batter must sit for one hour before cooking. You may use apricots, bananas, pears, or peaches as well as, or instead of, apples.

Summer Cottage

Aperitif: Rum punch or fruit punch
Fruit: Juicy peaches
Eggs: Hard-cooked egg pâté
Meat: French meat loaf
Fish: Mussels with tomatoes
Pâté: Liver pâté
Bread: French bread
Salad: Dandelion salad
Dessert: Fruit in Kirsch
Coffee: Iced coffee
Wine: Cider

Almost everything on this menu can be prepared the day before. The two pâtés should have 24 hours to chill, and the meat loaf can be served cold or reheated. Fruit in Kirsch can be chilled overnight. This leaves you with only the peaches, mussels, and salad to prepare when your guests arrive.

Discard any mussels that don't open in the oven. If you are collecting your own mussels, be sure that the surrounding water is clean. Substitute your favorite green salad if dandelion greens are not in season.

Thanksgiving Day

Aperitif: Russian apple
Fruit: Baked grapefruit
Eggs: Quiche Lorraine
Meat: Stuffed ham
Fish: Haddock fritters
Pâté: Rabbit pâté
Bread: Quick cheese bread or French bread
Salad: Belgian endive with beets
Dessert: Curacao Soufflé
Wine: Light red wine

The stuffed ham and the rabbit pâté can be prepared the day before. The bacon pieces for your Quiche Lorraine must be drained well on absorbent paper. The "Quick" cheese bread can be prepared in five minutes, but it takes an hour to bake.

The batter for haddock fritters must sit one hour before cooking. You'll need an assistant to fry the fish while you prepare the soufflé. For best flavor, let the endive marinate in its vinaigrette half an hour before adding the beets.

Christmas Holiday Open House

Aperitif: Bull-shot

Fruit: Apples

Eggs: Scrambled eggs with shrimp

Meat: Chicken pie or turkey pie

Pâté: Cognac and sherry pâté

Bread: Quick cheese bread

Fish: Fish with pasta shells

Salad: Green salad

Dessert: Pears with vanilla custard

Wine: Light red wine

The pâté should chill for 24 hours and you may want to prepare the meat pie filling and the pears at the same time. The cheese bread can be prepared very quickly but it needs an hour to bake. You'll need some help to prepare the fish while you cook the scrambled eggs and shrimp.

New Year's

Aperitif: Champagne and orange juice
Fruit: Rummy cantaloupe
Eggs: Lobster omelette
Meat: Roast pork with pineapple
Fish: Fish fillets on toast
Pâté: Hard-cooked egg pâté
Bread: Buttermilk biscuits
Salad: Rainbow salad
Dessert: Pineapple Chantilly
Wine: Champagne

This luxurious meal leaves you free to relax with your guests on New Year's morning. Prepare the cantaloupe, the pâté, the salad, and the chantilly the day before. If you serve the pork roast cold, it too can be prepared in advance; otherwise, allow three to four hours for roasting.

About half an hour before serving time, withdraw to the kitchen with an assistant to prepare the fish while you make the biscuits and omelette.

English Brunch

Aperitif: Bloody Mary

Fruit: Tipsy orange salad

Eggs: Omelette with cream and bacon

Meat: Corned beef with gherkin sauce

Fish: Grilled smelts or herring

Bread: Muffins

Cheese Tray

Salad: Green salad

Dessert: Tropical cream

Tea or Irish coffee

Beer

The orange salad and the tropical cream can be prepared the day before. One hour before, arrange your cheese tray so that the cheese can ripen while you begin preparing the muffins. They'll need half an hour to bake. Be sure the omelette eggs are at room temperature or let them sit 20 minutes in a bowl of warm water.

Salt the smelts half an hour before grilling and pre-heat the broiler. You'll want some help to prepare the salad while you cook the omelette.

French Brunch

Aperitif: Champagne and orange juice
Fruit: Tipsy orange salad
Eggs: Eggs in red wine
Meat: Chicken in white wine
Pâté: Pork rillettes
Vegetables: Stuffed tomatoes
Salad: Dandelion salad
Cheese Tray
Dessert: Apricot Barquettes
Bread: Croissants
Wine: White wine

The orange salad, pork rillettes, and stuffed tomatoes can be prepared the day before. If your croissants are a day old, freshen them in a wet brown paper bag for ten minutes in a 350° oven. Substitute your favorite green salad if dandelions are not in season.

One hour before serving time, mix the barquette batter and prepare the cheese tray so that your cheeses can ripen to their best flavor. Prepare the eggs at the last minute, while the chicken and mushrooms are simmering. You will need the nelp of a friend now to fry the barquettes.

Italian Meatless Brunch

Aperitif: Screwdriver
Fruit: Large fruit plate
Eggs: Crêpes milanaises
Vegetables: Eggplant with butterfly noodles
Fish: Squid with tomato and red pepper or
  Scallop soufflé
Bread: Brioche endimanchée
Salad: Green peppers meridional
Dessert: Apple and pear upside-down cake
Coffee: Espresso
Wine: Italian white or red

If you're slicing the fruit, sprinkle the pieces with lemon juice so they don't discolor. Marinate the squid and the green pepper for 24 hours. The eggplant mixture can also be prepared the day before (and it must have an hour to simmer). Prepare the crêpes and the brioche batter at least two hours ahead of time. Be sure your soufflé eggs are at room temperature or let them sit 20 minutes in warm water.

When the soufflé and the brioche are in the oven, begin preparing the crêpes. Since your oven will be fully occupied, keep the crêpes warm on the stove on an ovenproof platter placed over a skillet of simmering water. Recruit a guest or member of the family to prepare the upside-down cake. It will bake while the main dishes are being served.

Drinks

Drink recipes are for one person

Bloody Mary

2 ounces (50 ml) vodka
6 ounces (175 ml) tomato juice
A few drops of lemon juice
6 drops of Worcestershire sauce
3 drops of Tabasco
Salt and pepper

Pour the vodka over ice into a large tumbler. Add the tomato juice and the rest of the ingredients. Stir well.

Champagne and Orange Juice

1½ ounces (40 ml) orange juice
1½ ounces (40 ml) champagne

Pour the orange juice into a refrigerated champagne glass. Add well-chilled champagne.

If you're watching your budget, sparkling cider may be substituted for the champagne.

"Lea and Perrins" synonymous with Worcestershire Sauce *(pronounced 'Wuster') is a valuable asset in the kitchen — a condiment mysterious and potent, an ancient mingling of vinegar, molasses, anchovies, tamarinds, garlic and spices.*

Brandy Eggnog

"I never drink anything stronger than gin before breakfast" — W.C. Fields

1½ ounces (40 ml) brandy
1 egg
6 ounces (175 ml) milk
½ teaspoon (2 ml) sugar
Nutmeg

Mix the ingredients thoroughly in a blender. Pour into a large glass and sprinkle with nutmeg.

Port Flip

2 ounces (50 ml) port
1 teaspoon (5 ml) powdered sugar
1 egg

Combine the ingredients in a cocktail shaker. Shake well. Strain and pour into a cocktail glass. Grate a little nutmeg over the top.

For an even smoother port flip make the drink in the blender.

Red Eye

1 ounce (25 ml) tomato juice
4 ounces (100 ml) beer

Pour the tomato juice into a large glass. Top up with beer and stir. Serve very cold.

Rum Punch

2 ounces (50 ml) white rum
6 ounces (175 ml) sweetened grapefruit juice
Four-Spices (Quatre Épices) to taste

Half fill a large glass with crushed ice. Add the rum, the grapefruit juice and spices. Stir.

There is no medical substantiation for the benefits of the "hair of the dog" other than the temporary relief of continued anaesthesis.

Vichy Vodka

Even the Romans knew better. They imbibed "hair of the dog" only as an antidote for dog-bite — the hair to be taken from the same beast (a task which called for great courage under the circumstances) and also to be burnt (which called for a strong digestion).

1½ ounces (40 ml) vodka
6 ounces (175 ml) Vichy water
1 teaspoon lemon juice

Pour the vodka over ice into a large glass. Add the Vichy water and lemon juice. Stir well.

Bull-Shot

4 ounces (100 ml) canned consommé
1½ ounces (40 ml) vodka

Make the consommé according to the instructions on the can. Pour the vodka into a glass and add the consommé. Serve over ice.

Variation:

1 ounce (25 ml) brandy
or
1 ounce (25 ml) rum
4 ounces (100 ml) consommé

Variation: Use a beef boullion cube.

Russian Apple

2 ounces (50 ml) vodka
4 ounces (100 ml) apple juice
1 cinnamon stick

Half fill a large glass with crushed ice. Pour in the vodka and the apple juice. Stir gently.

Add a cinnamon stick as a muddler.

Screwdriver

2 ounces (50 ml) vodka
6 ounces (175 ml) orange juice
1 slice of lime

Pour the vodka over ice into a large glass. Add the orange juice. Stir well and garnish with a slice of lime.

Fruit

All recipes serve four

Rummy Cantaloupe

1 cantaloupe
1 small tin of pineapple slices
¾ cup (175 ml) white sugar
4 ounces (100 ml) water
4 ounces (100 ml) rum

Cut the top off a cantaloupe. Remove the seeds and discard them. Then scoop out all the fruit being careful not to puncture the skin.

Bring the sugar, water and the juice from the tinned pineapple to the boiling point and simmer for a minute.

Let chill and add the rum.

Cut the cantaloupe flesh which has been removed from the shell and the pineapple slices into very small pieces and add to the syrup.

Fill the melon with this mixture, replace the cap, and chill for a couple of hours or until time to serve.

The cantaloupe once picked does not develop further in flavor and sweetness. The trick is to select a good one with a sweet, musky fragrance, the veining prominent against the skin and a slightly sunken scar at the stem end.

Tipsy Orange Salad

4 oranges
4 tablespoons (50 ml) white sugar
1 ounce (25 ml) kirsch

Peel the oranges. Cut into slices as thin as possible. Arrange in a fruit dish. Sprinkle with sugar and kirsch. Serve very cold.

Baked Grapefruit

*Our drug-oriented
society seems to
have overlooked
a valuable
resource. Fennel
not only stimulates
the appetite, aids
the digestion,
disperses flatulence
but eases the eyes.*

2 grapefruit
½ cup (125 ml) white sugar
4 teaspoons (20 ml) butter

Cut the grapefruit in half and loosen the sections.
Place a piece of butter in the center of each half
and cover the cut surface of the fruit with sugar.

Butter an oven-proof dish and place the 4 grapefruit halves in it. Glaze the halves in the oven until
they are hot and bubbly — around 10 minutes at
350°F (180°C).

Pour any syrup in the baking dish over the
grapefruit halves before serving.

Variation: Add a spoonful of rum to each
grapefruit half.

Variation: Remove the grapefruit segments and
toss them with a bit of cinnamon and brown
sugar. Fill the empty halves with the mixture, dot
with butter and sprinkle a few crushed fennel
seeds over the top. Broil.

Juicy Peaches

4 peaches
Water
Sugar to taste

Wash the peaches and drop them in gently boiling
water. Simmer 4 - 5 minutes.

Drain, peel, and cut in half from the stem end
down. Remove the pit.

Arrange the peaches in a serving dish. Sprinkle
with sugar and serve.

Variation: Before serving the peaches flavor
them with brandy or kirsch — 1 ounce (25 ml) per
serving.

Breads

All recipes serve four

Brioche Endimanchée

1 cup (250 ml) sifted all-purpose flour
¾ cup (175 ml) white sugar
Grated rind of half a lemon
3 eggs, separated
3 tablespoons (45 ml) melted butter

Mix together the flour, sugar, grated rind, and the yolks of the eggs. Add the melted butter to the mixture.

Beat the egg whites to soft peaks and blend with the rest of the ingredients.

Turn the batter into a buttered 8-inch square pan (20 cm) and bake for 1 hour at 350°F (180°C).

Eggs are best beaten when at room temperature. If you've forgotten to take them out of the refrigerator in time, place them in a bowl of warm water for a few moments.

Buttermilk Biscuits

¾ teaspoon (3 ml) baking soda
1½ cups (350 ml) buttermilk
3 cups (750 ml) sifted all-purpose flour
3 teaspoons (15 ml) baking powder
½ teaspoon (2 ml) salt
2 tablespoons (30 ml) shortening
2 tablespoons (30 ml) butter

Dissolve the baking soda in the buttermilk.

Combine the dry ingredients in a bowl. Cut in the butter and shortening with a pastry blender or 2 knives. Add the buttermilk and baking soda and mix in with a fork.

Form the dough into a ball then pat it down to ½ inch thickness (approximately 1 cm) with your hands.

Cut into rounds, with a cutter or with a glass dipped in flour. Arrange on a greased cookie sheet.

Bake at 450°F (230°C) for 12 to 15 minutes or until lightly browned. Yield 18 to 24 biscuits.

Muffins

1 egg
1 cup (250 ml) milk
¼ cup (75ml) oil
2 cups (500 ml) all-purpose flour
¼ cup (75 ml) granulated sugar
1 teaspoon (5 ml) salt
3 teaspoons (15 ml) baking powder
½ cup (150 ml) raisins

Beat the egg and blend with the milk and oil.

Sift together the flour, sugar, salt, and baking powder. Add the raisins.

Combine the dry and liquid mixtures and blend until smooth.

Grease 12 muffin tins and fill two-thirds full. Bake 20-25 minutes in a 400°F (200°C) oven.

Sad to say, a warm, speckled brown egg does not taste any better nor is it better for you than that clinical white one. It was merely laid by a different breed of hen, probably a Columbia Rock or a Rhode Island Red. The flavor depends on the freshness of the egg and the diet of the chicken.

Quick Cheese Bread

2 cups (50 ml) all-purpose flour
4 teaspoons (20 ml) baking powder
½ teaspoon (2.5 ml) salt
1 cup (250 ml) grated cheese
2 eggs
1 cup (250 ml) milk
¼ cup (75 ml) oil

Sift together the flour, baking powder, and salt. Add the grated cheese.

Beat together the eggs, milk, and oil and add them to the dry ingredients. Blend delicately.

Grease a bread loaf tin and turn the mixture into it. Bake 55 minutes in a 350°F (180°C) oven.

Eggs & cheese

All recipes serve four

Crêpes Milanaises

½ cup (125 ml) sifted all-purpose flour
1 egg, beaten
1¼ cups (300 ml) half milk, half water
2 tablespoons (30 ml) grated gruyère cheese
2 teaspoons (10 ml) tomato paste
Salt and pepper
Butter

Mix together the flour, egg, water and milk. Let stand at least 2 hours.

Add the grated cheese, tomato paste, and salt and pepper.

Heat a little butter in a medium-sized frying pan or crêpe pan. Pour in about 3 tablespoons (45 ml) of batter and tilt the pan so the batter covers the bottom completely.

Brown each crêpe on one side only. When the other side is dry, do not turn the crêpe over but roll it up on itself in the pan and slide it onto a warm serving plate.

These crêpes go especially well with baked fish.

In order to ease the performance of making crêpes, melt a lump of sweet butter in a small saucepan. Dip a brush or piece of paper into the warm clear butter and rub it around the crêpe pan. This gives you just the right amount of fat and you don't have to wait for the butter to melt and heat up for each crêpe.

Scotch Eggs

In all probability your grandmother omitted to teach you how to boil an egg. Here's the best way. Cover the eggs with cold water, bring them to a boil, reduce the heat to a simmer and cook 2-3 minutes for a soft yolk, 5 minutes for a firm yolk. Compensate in the length of cooking time if you took the eggs straight from the refrigerator or have an extra large egg.

4 eggs, hard-cooked
Flour
Salt and pepper
¾ pound (approximately 350 g) sausage meat
1 egg, beaten
Bread crumbs
Oil for deep frying

Shell the 4 eggs and roll them in flour seasoned with salt and pepper.

Divide the sausage meat into 4 equal parts and coat the eggs with it. (Dip your fingers in flour to handle the meat more easily.)

Dip each ball in the beaten egg, then in crumbs. Let stand half an hour before deep frying.

Lower the balls into very hot deep fat, turn them and cook until well browned. Drain briefly on absorbent paper. Cut in two, lengthwise, and serve at once.

Eggs Provençale

2 tablespoons (30 ml) oil
6 medium-sized tomatoes, peeled
2 cloves of garlic, minced
3 sprigs of parsley
Salt and pepper
Herbs of Provence (bay leaves, rosemary, savory)
4 eggs

Heat the oil in a frying pan.

Cut the tomatoes into large pieces and add with minced garlic and parsley to the pan. Add salt and pepper and herbs to taste. Sauté 10 minutes over medium heat.

Mash the tomatoes with a fork. Break the eggs over the tomatoes and continue cooking gently until the whites are firm.

Eggs au Gratin

8 tablespoons (125 ml) grated gruyère cheese
4 eggs
1 generous cup (250 ml) fresh cream (35%)
2 tablespoons (30 ml) butter
Salt and pepper

Butter an oven-proof dish. Sprinkle half the grated gruyère on the bottom. Break the eggs over the cheese. Cover with cream, making sure it is evenly distributed over the whole dish. Sprinkle with the remaining half of the grated cheese and dot with butter.

Bake 15 minutes at 325°F (170°C). If you prefer well-done eggs lengthen the cooking time.

Eggs in Red Wine

4 slices French bread
2 tablespoons (30 ml) vegetable oil
4 tablespoons (50 ml) butter
4 tablespoons (50 ml) sifted all-purpose flour
2 cups (500 ml) red wine
½ cup (100 ml) hot water
4 eggs

Brown the bread slices in oil. Drain on absorbent paper then place them on a serving platter.

Melt the butter in a saucepan. Blend in the flour.

In another pan, bring the wine to the boiling point, then add the butter and flour mixture little by little. Add the hot water and stir until the sauce becomes smooth. Pour the sauce over the fried bread.

Poach or fry the eggs, whichever you prefer, and arrange them on top.

How do you make fried eggs? Everyone has a favorite way but we recommend melting the butter without letting it brown, breaking the eggs into the pan, covering and letting cook over low heat for 3-4 minutes.

Scrambled Eggs with Shrimp

Anchovies are small relatives of the herring. Less familiar to North Americans than to Europeans, their distinctive flavor adds much to certain sauces and meat dishes and is complementary to tomatoes, eggs and onions.

1 slice of bread per person
1 tube of anchovy paste
2 tablespoons (30 ml) butter
1 4-ounce tin (approximately 150 g) shrimp
10 eggs
Pepper
2 tablespoons (30 ml) butter
8 anchovies

Fry the slices of bread in butter and drain on absorbent paper. Spread with anchovy paste and keep warm.

Melt 2 tablespoons (30 ml) butter in a thick-bottomed pan. Add the drained shrimp.

Beat the eggs, add the pepper and several pieces of butter and blend with the shrimp. Stir over a low heat until just set.

Cover the fried bread with the scrambled egg mixture. Garnish each serving with 2 anchovy fillets.

Serve at once.

Eggs Pizou

6 eggs, hard-cooked
4 tablespoons (50 ml) fresh cream (35%)
¼ teaspoon (1 ml) tarragon finely chopped
¼ pound (approximately 125 g) mushrooms finely
    chopped
2 tablespoons (30 ml) butter
2 cups (500 ml) tomato sauce, canned or home-
    made (see page 123)
Anchovy fillets

Shell the eggs and cut in two, lengthwise.

Remove the yolks and mash them with a fork.
Add the cream, the tarragon and the mushrooms.
Stuff the eggs with this mixture.

Arrange the egg halves in a lightly buttered
baking dish. Cover with tomato sauce.

Bake in a 350°F (180°C) oven for 5 minutes.

Just before serving, garnish with a few
anchovies.

Stuffed Eggs

4 eggs, hard-cooked
4 anchovies, finely chopped
Pepper
1 cup (250 ml) mayonnaise (see page 124)

Shell the eggs and cut them in two, lengthwise.

Remove the yolks. Keep two in reserve. Mash the other yolks with the chopped anchovies and add pepper. Stuff each egg with this mixture.

Cover with mayonnaise and arrange on a small serving platter.

Put the two remaining yolks through a coarse sieve and sprinkle over the top.

Variation: You can substitute for the anchovies 2 or 3 fillets of finely chopped marinated herring, or 2 to 3 tablespoons (30 - 45 ml) of lobster, crab, salmon or canned tuna fish.

Egg and Ham Croquettes

6 eggs, hard-cooked
⅓ pound (approximately 175 g) cooked ham
1 tablespoon (15 ml) butter
2 tablespoons (30 ml) flour
1 generous cup (250 ml) milk
Salt and pepper
1 egg yolk
Flour
1 beaten egg
Bread crumbs
Oil for deep frying
1 cup (250 ml) tomato sauce (see page 123)

Shell the eggs and chop them together with the ham.

Melt the butter in a double boiler and stir in the flour. Add the milk, salt and pepper, and stir until thickened. Add the egg yolk, then the ham and hard-cooked egg mixture. Let cool and shape into croquettes.

Dip each croquette in flour, then in the beaten egg, then in the bread crumbs. Deep fry in oil until golden.

Cover with tomato sauce.

For a perfect hard-cooked egg use method as for soft-cooked but extend the simmering time to 15 minutes. Stop the cooking by immersing the egg in cold water at once, which makes the egg easier to shell and prevents a dark ring from forming around the yolk.

Omelette with Cream and Bacon

2 medium-sized potatoes
¼ pound (approximately 125 g) bacon
½ cup (100 ml) fresh cream (35%)
4 tablespoons (60 ml) grated gruyère cheese
4 eggs
1 tablespoon (15 ml) water
Salt and pepper

Cube the potatoes and cut the bacon into small pieces. Cook them together in a frying pan or large omelette pan for about 10 minutes.

Heat the cream and cheese together in a saucepan over low heat.

Beat the eggs and add the water, salt and pepper. Turn into the frying pan with the bacon and potatoes. Cook several minutes over medium high heat. Loosen the edges, lift up the mixture and tip the pan so the uncooked eggs can run underneath. Shake the pan to prevent sticking.

When the omelette is almost done (still creamy) pour on the cream and melted cheese.

Fold the omelette as you slip it out of the pan onto a warm platter.

Serve at once.

Lobster Omelette

1 tablespoon (15 ml) butter
1 tin of lobster, drained and broken into pieces
1 teaspoon (5 ml) chopped shallots
Salt and pepper
2 tablespoons (30 ml) Cognac
1 tablespoon (15 ml) chopped parsley
3 tablespoons (45 ml) fresh cream (35%)
6 eggs
1 tablespoon (15 ml) water
2 tablespoons (30 ml) butter
2 tablespoons (30 ml) grated gruyère cheese

Eggs become tough and unpleasant when cooked for too long or over too high a heat.

In a saucepan, melt the butter and gently brown the lobster and the shallots. Season with salt and pepper.

Add the Cognac and stir to make a sauce with the juice and crusty bits.

Flame this, (see page 64) then add the chopped parsley and the cream and blend well. Set aside.

In a large bowl, beat the eggs and add the water and some salt and pepper.

Melt 2 tablespoons (30 ml) of butter in a frying pan or large omelette pan and allow it to get bubbly hot. Pour in the eggs and proceed as for the omelette on the previous page.

While the omelette is still soft, pour the lobster mixture on top, sprinkle with the grated gruyère.

Fold the omelette as you slip it out of the pan. Serve at once.

Omelette with Croutons

2 slices of stale bread
Oil for frying
5 eggs
1 tablespoon (15 ml) water
Salt and pepper
2 tablespoons (30 ml) butter

Cube the bread. Brown in hot oil. Remove the croutons and keep them in a warm oven.

Beat the eggs in a bowl and add the water and salt and pepper.

Cook the omelette (see page 52) in a frying pan or a large omelette pan.

Place the croutons on the top of the omelette before folding it onto a warmed serving platter.

Onion Pie

1 cup (approximately 250 ml) sliced onions
2 tablespoons (30 ml) butter
3 eggs
Salt and pepper
A pinch of dry mustard
1 partially-baked pie shell (see page 126)
2 tablespoons (30 ml) grated cheddar cheese
1 cup (250 ml) fresh cream (35%)
4 slices mozarella cheese
3 slices of bacon cut in half

Black peppercorns are picked when green, left a few days to ferment, then dried until shrivelled and darkened in color. The entire peppercorn including the husk is used.

Sauté sliced onions in butter over medium heat until golden, about 10 minutes.

Beat the eggs. Season with salt and pepper.

Sprinkle the mustard into the bottom of partially-baked pie shell. Add the grated cheddar cheese and onions, then the eggs beaten together with the cream. Cover with slices of mozarella cheese.

Bake 30 minutes at 325°F (170°C).

While this is cooking, fry the bacon until crisp. Drain on absorbent paper.

When the pie is out of the oven, arrange the bacon slices in a star shape on the top. Serve at once.

Cheese and Ham Soufflé

To scald milk, heat over direct heat or in the top of a double boiler over, not in, hot water. Milk is scalded when tiny bubbles form around the edge of the pan.

1 cup (250 ml) milk
2 tablespoons (30 ml) butter
2 tablespoons (30 ml) flour
4 tablespoons (60 ml) grated gruyère cheese or Parmesan cheese
¼ pound (approximately 125 g) chopped ham
3 egg yolks
Salt and pepper
4 egg whites

Scald the milk.

In a double boiler, melt the butter and stir in the flour. Let cook for a few moments.

Blend in the hot milk. The sauce should be thick but not gummy. Add a little more scalded milk if necessary.

Fold in the cheese and ham, and the egg yolks one at a time. Season with salt and pepper. Mix well. Allow to cool 10 minutes.

Beat the egg whites to form stiff peaks and fold into the mixture.

Turn into a 1½ quart (1.5 l) soufflé dish with a buttered paper collar.

Bake 25 minutes at 350°F (180°C) then increase the heat to 400°F (200°C) and bake another 5 minutes.

Quiche Lorraine

6 slices of bacon
or
¼ pound (approximately 125 g) bacon slab
1 unbaked pie shell (see page 126)
3 eggs
1 generous cup (250 ml) fresh cream (35%)
Salt and pepper
3 tablespoons (45 ml) grated gruyère cheese

Dice the sliced bacon or cube the bacon slab and sauté in butter until it changes color. Turn into the unbaked pie shell.

Beat the eggs. Add the cream, salt and pepper, and grated cheese. Pour over the bacon.

Bake 30 minutes or until puffed and lightly browned at 400°F (200°C).

A valley in Switzerland which lends its name to gruyère, that waxy, dryish cheese with a pungent, distinctive flavor which melts deliciously. Buy it by the piece and grate it as you need it.

Meat dishes

All recipes serve four

Bacon, English Style

1 pound (approximately 500 g) bacon
4 tomatoes
or
½ pound (approximately 250 g) mushrooms

Cut the bacon in bite-size pieces. Fry it, pressing down on the fat parts with a fork.

Remove the bacon from the pan, drain on absorbent paper and keep warm in the oven.

Slice the tomatoes, if used, or chop the mushrooms and sauté in the bacon fat for 15 minutes.

Pour the tomatoes or mushrooms over the bacon and serve hot.

To skin, or not to skin a tomato? The skin contains valuable vitamins; therefore keep them on unless the dish demands a certain delicacy.

Corned Beef with Gherkin Sauce

1 onion
2 tablespoons (30 ml) butter
1 tablespoon (15 ml) sifted all-purpose flour
1 cup (250 ml) hot water
5 or 6 gherkins cut in thin round slices
1 tablespoon (15 ml) cider vinegar
1 12 ounce (350 g) tin of corned beef

Slice or chop the onion. Sauté it in butter until it changes color. Add the flour, stir and brown. Thin with hot water. Cook 5 - 8 minutes, stirring constantly.

Add the gherkins, the vinegar and the corned beef broken in pieces. Stir and heat until piping hot.

Pork and Beans with Beer

Of all the pork and beans recipes we have known, this one, from publicist Jacques Bouchard, seems to us by far the best. He has agreed to our passing it on to you and we thank him for it.

1 pound (approximately 500 g) dry white beans
1 12-ounce (350 ml) bottle of beer
4½ cups (approximately 1 *l*) water
1 pound (approximately 500 g) unsalted pork fat
1 pound (approximately 500 g) ham
6 slices of bacon
2 onions, chopped
½ cup (125 ml) molasses
½ cup (125 ml) maple syrup
2 whole cloves
Pepper
1 tablespoon (15 ml) dry mustard

Wash the beans well. Soak them in the water and beer for 12 hours or overnight. Then simmer in the same liquid for an hour. Skim.

In an ovenproof ceramic or stoneware pot, place the pork fat, the ham cut in large cubes, the bacon, the onions, the molasses, maple syrup, cloves, pepper and mustard. Add the beans with their juice. Bake 3 hours at 350°F (180°C).

10 minutes before the end of the cooking time, stir the dish with a spoon to bring the meat to the surface. Place under the broiler for 10 minutes to brown the meat.

Dried beans need to be soaked before cooking. A quick soak method allows 3 cups of water to 1 cup of beans. Bring to the boil, boil rapidly for 2 minutes. Remove from the heat and let stand 1 hour. Bring beans to a boil and simmer gently ½ hour if the beans are to be baked further, or for 1 hour if they are to be served as is.

Chicken in White Wine

"To flame" requires practice and all too often results in a pathetic flicker or a frantic call to the fire department. To be flamed gently helps to warm the food. Measure the liquor into a warmed ladle, pour it into the dish, set alight with a long match . . . and stand back.

1 roasting chicken, 3 to 4 pounds (approximately 1.5 to 2 kg)
2 tablespoons (30 ml) flour
4 tablespoons (60 ml) butter
2 onions, minced
1 tablespoon (15 ml) Cognac
Salt and pepper
1 cup (approximately 250 ml) dry white wine
Small bouquet garni (thyme, parsley, bay leaf)
½ pound (approximately 250 g) mushrooms, sliced
¼ cup (50 ml) fresh cream (35%)
2 egg yolks, beaten

Cut the chicken in serving pieces; dust with flour.

Melt the butter in a large kettle and sauté the minced onions together with the chicken until golden. Sprinkle on the Cognac and set it alight. When the flames subside, add the salt, pepper, wine and bouquet garni and simmer 30 minutes. Add the mushrooms, stir and let simmer 30 minutes.

Mix the cream with the egg yolks, add to sauce and heat through before serving.

Stuffed Ham

7 pounds (approximately 3 to 3.5 kg) ready-to-
   serve boneless ham
A slice of bread with the crusts removed
¼ cup (50 ml) milk
½ pound (approximately 250 g) mushrooms,
   finely chopped
½ green pepper, finely chopped
Chervil, tarragon, rosemary and sage
2 shallots, finely chopped
Salt and pepper
¼ pound (approximately 125 g) raisins
3 tablespoons (45 ml) Dijon-type mustard
White sugar
Whole cloves

Tarragon, the aristocratic herb of haute cuisine can be used generously in salads and sauces when fresh, but should be added with discretion when dried for it tends to be too assertive.

Cut off a small piece about ½ cup (125 ml) from the ham and chop finely.

Soak the bread in the milk. Add the chopped ham and the mushrooms, green pepper, herbs, shallots, garlic, all finely chopped. Season with salt and pepper and add the raisins. Mix thoroughly.

Heat the ham in a 325°F (160°C) oven for 45 minutes. Cut the ham in half lengthwise and place the stuffing in the middle. Roll it up and tie it. Cut the fat in diamond shapes. Coat with mustard. Place in a 400°F (200°C) oven for 10 minutes.

Remove the ham from the oven and roll it in the sugar, making sure the whole surface is covered. Put it in a 350°F (180°C) oven for 30 minutes. Turn it from time to time.

Spread with sugar again, stud with cloves and put back in a 350°F (180°C) oven for a final 10 minutes. Chill until serving time.

French Meat Loaf

Pliny recommended, among other delicacies, the snout and foot of hippopotamus to increase sexual potency. Easier to come by and with reportedly equally pleasureable results is a garlic bud.

6 tablespoons (90 ml) butter
1 tablespoon (15 ml) flour
3 tablespoons (45 ml) tomato paste
½ cup (125 ml) beef stock
1 pound (approximately 500 g) minced beef
Garlic, crushed
Parsley, chopped
Salt and pepper
1 egg, beaten

Melt the butter in a double boiler and add the flour. Blend well. Add the tomato paste and moisten with the beef stock, stirring constantly. Simmer for 10 minutes.

Add the minced beef, a trace of crushed garlic, the chopped parsley and salt and pepper. Simmer for 10 minutes. Remove from the stove and let cool.

Blend in the beaten egg and turn the mixture into a buttered mold.

Set the mold in a pan of water and bake for about 40 minutes at 325°F (170°C). Remove from the mold and serve sliced hot or cold.

Chicken Pie

1 roasting chicken, 3 to 4 pounds (approximately 1.5 to 2 kg)
3 tablespoons (45 ml) butter
2 medium-sized onions, finely chopped
Salt and pepper
1 cup (approximately 250 ml) broth made from the chicken giblets
Small bouquet garni (thyme, parsley, bay leaf)
3 medium-sized tomatoes, peeled and chopped
¼ pound (approximately 125 g) mushrooms
1 tablespoon (15 ml) butter
A few drops of lemon juice
1 slice of cooked ham cubed
2 hard-cooked eggs sliced
1 tablespoon (15 ml) herbs, (parsley, thyme and chives) finely chopped
1 teaspoon (5 ml) cornstarch
Pie pastry dough (see page 126)

Several garlic buds were found in the tomb of Tutankhamen dating from about 1358 B.C. which just shows that the Egyptians knew a thing or two.

Cut the chicken into 8 pieces. Melt the butter in a saucepan. Brown the chicken and the onions. Season with salt and pepper.

Remove the chicken and set aside. Make a sauce by adding the chicken broth. Add the bouquet garni, the chopped tomatoes, and the chicken pieces. Cover and simmer ½ hour.

Take the chicken from the bone and transfer it and the sauce to an oven-proof dish. Add the mushrooms, minced and sautéed in butter, the lemon juice, the ham, the sliced hard-cooked eggs, and the finely chopped herbs. Blend the cornstarch with cold water, stir into the mixture.

Prepare the pastry dough and cover the dish with it. Secure it to the edge of the dish with a little water or egg white.

Make a paper chimney in the center and bake in a 350°F (180°C) oven for 30 minutes.

Spiced Sausage and Potato Stew

2 medium-sized onions
2 tablespoons (30 ml) butter
1 tablespoon (15 ml) flour
1 cup (250 ml) water
8 medium-sized potatoes peeled and cut in pieces
Salt and pepper
4 spiced sausages
2 tablespoons (30 ml) cider or wine vinegar

Chop the onions and sauté in butter until they change color. Add the flour and blend well. Stir in the water to make a smooth sauce.

Add the potatoes. Season with salt and pepper. Simmer for ½ hour.

Cook the sausages in butter so they are brown on all sides, and add to the potatoes and sauce.

Just before serving, stir in the vinegar.

Beef Rissoles

Pie pastry dough (see page 126)
2 tablespoons (30 ml) pork fat cut in cubes
1 teaspoon (5 ml) butter
1 onion, finely chopped
1 small carrot, finely chopped
¾ pound (approximately 350 g) minced beef
2 tablespoons (30 ml) sifted all-purpose flour
1 cup (250 ml) beef stock
1 teaspoon (5 ml) powdered beef concentrate
Salt and pepper
1 egg, beaten
Bread crumbs
Oil for deep frying

Prepare the pie pastry dough.

Sauté the cubed pork fat in butter.

Add the finely chopped onion and carrot and cook until the onion is golden. Add the minced meat and flour and brown, stirring constantly. Add the beef stock to make a sauce; stir in the beef concentrate and salt and pepper. Let cool.

Cut the pastry in 4 circles, 4 inches (10 cm) in diameter.

Place the minced beef stuffing onto the center of the circles, fold the edges together, moisten with water and seal well. Brush with beaten egg.

Roll the rissoles in bread crumbs and fry in deep fat. Drain on absorbent paper. Keep warm until serving time.

Beef rissoles are generally served with a tomato sauce (see page 123).

Roast Pork with Pineapple

In the West Indies a pineapple hung at the entrance to a hut as a sign of welcome. A custom brought back to Europe where many a carved stone pineapple stands majestic on a gate post.

4 pounds (approximately 2 kg) roast pork (shoulder or loin)
3 tablespoons (45 ml) butter
Salt and pepper
1 large tin pineapple slices

Brown the roast on all sides in butter in a large pot. Add salt and pepper, cover and cook for 2 hours or so.

Use the juice from the tinned pineapple to baste from time to time. When the roast is done remove from the pot, let cool and slice.

Reheat the pot and brown the pineapple slices in the pan juices.

Alternate the slices of warm pineapple with the slices of cold roast pork on a serving platter.

Fish dishes

All recipes serve four

Haddock Fritters

1½ pounds (approximately 700 g) haddock
  fillets
Court-bouillon (see page 123)
2 tablespoons (30 ml) lemon juice
Pepper
½ cup (125 ml) sifted all-purpose flour
1 egg, separated
1 teaspoon oil (5 ml)
1 teaspoon (5 ml) baking powder
4 tablespoons (60 ml) warm water
Oil for deep frying

Poach the fish for 15 minutes in court-bouillon.
Then cut the fish in bite-size pieces, sprinkle with
lemon juice and pepper.

Put the flour in a bowl. Make a well in the
center. Place in it the egg yolk; 1 teaspoon oil (5
ml) and the baking powder. Blend, and thin with
the warm water. Add the egg white beaten to stiff
peaks. Let stand one hour.

Dip the pieces of fish in this batter. Lower into
hot deep fat and brown well.

These fritters may be served with tomato sauce
(see page 123).

"We have
observed in France
that those who live
almost entirely on
shellfish and
fish. . . are more
ardent in love than
others. In fact, we
ourselves feel more
amorously
inclined during
Lent" — Dr
Nicholas Venette,
17th century
writer.

Cream of Cod

8 potatoes
2 tablespoons (30 ml) butter
½ cup (125 ml) milk, scalded (see page 56)
2 pounds (approximately 1 kg) cod fillets
Court-bouillon (see page 123)
6 cloves of garlic, finely minced
¼ cup (50 ml) oil

Cook the potatoes in salted boiling water. Drain, remove skins and purée them through a food mill.

Put the purée back on low heat. Make a well in the middle and place the butter in it. Beat thoroughly and add scalded milk little by little until the purée is creamy.

Meanwhile, poach the fish in court-bouillon for 15 minutes. Drain, skin, and blend with the potato purée.

Add the minced garlic, then the oil drop by drop while beating the mixture, as you would in making a mayonnaise. (see page 124). Serve warm.

Variation: Salt cod is a delicious substitute but must be soaked in water overnight to reduce the salty flavor.

Squid with Tomato and Red Pepper

2 tins of squid
1 tablespoon (15 ml) wine vinegar
3 tablespoons (45 ml) olive oil
Salt and pepper
2 tablespoons (30 ml) tomato sauce (see page 123)
1 sweet red pepper
Parsley, finely chopped

A squid is not the most alluring of creatures — resembling a gelatinous bag out of which sprouts an ugly head and gangling tentacles — but then beauty's only skin deep.

Drain the contents of the tins of squid and put in a bowl.

Blend the vinegar, oil, salt and pepper and tomato sauce. Pour over the squid and mix well.

Add the pepper, washed, seeded, and cut in pieces, and the parsley.

Mix all again. Serve chilled.

The flavor of this Mediterranean dish is improved if it is allowed to marinate overnight. It is served as an antipasto or salad.

Tuna Loaf

If it is imperative for the aesthetic effect that your egg-yolks are centered in the whites, stir the eggs around gently several times during the first few minutes of simmering.

4 large potatoes
2 slices of bread
½ cup (125 ml) milk
1 tin of tuna
1 tablespoon (15 ml) tomato paste
Mayonnaise (see page 124)
2 eggs, hard-cooked and sliced
2 medium tomatoes
Parsley, chopped

Cook the potatoes in salted, boiling water. Remove skins and mash.

Soak the bread in milk and add to the potatoes along with the tuna and tomato paste. Mix thoroughly.

Press the mixture carefully into a mold, cover, and refrigerate 12 hours.

Unmold and serve with a mayonnaise. Garnish with egg slices, fresh tomatoes and parsley. Slice and serve.

Fish with Pasta Shells

1 tablespoon (15 ml) butter
1 tablespoon (15 ml) flour
½ cup (125 ml) water or vegetable water
Salt and pepper
¼ pound (approximately 125 g) pasta shells
¼ pound (approximately 125 g) any kind of leftover cooked fish
2 tablespoons (30 ml) melted butter
Bread crumbs

Melt the butter in a double boiler and stir in the flour. Cook for a few minutes. Blend in the warm water or vegetable water. Beat with a wire whisk to prevent lumps from forming. Add salt and pepper and cook 5 minutes.

Cook the pasta shells 20 minutes in salted, boiling water (or follow directions on the package). Drain.

Combine the pasta, the cooked fish, and the sauce. Turn into a baking dish. Cover with bread crumbs tossed in melted butter and bake 10 minutes in a 400°F (200°C) oven.

Fish with Mashed Potatoes

1 pound (approximately 500 g) fish, any kind
Court-bouillon (see page 123)
5 potatoes
2 tablespoons (30 ml) butter
½ cup (125 ml) milk
2 eggs, hard-cooked
Salt and pepper
½ cup (approximately 125 ml) grated gruyère
  cheese
Bread crumbs
2 tablespoons (30 ml) butter

Poach fish 15 minutes in court-bouillon.

Cook potatoes in salted, boiling water, remove skins and mash. Stir in butter and milk.

Shell the eggs and cut into slices.

Flake the cooked fish, taking care to remove the bones.

In an oven-proof dish, spread a layer of mashed potato, then a layer of flaked fish and one of sliced egg. Salt and pepper each layer. Top with a layer of mashed potatoes. Cover the whole mixture with grated cheese and bread crumbs and dot with butter.

Brown 20 minutes in a 350°F (180°C) oven.

Variation: This dish can be varied by replacing the grated cheese with a white sauce.

Mussels with Tomatoes

¼ cup (approximately 50 ml) raw rice
2 tablespoons (30 ml) oil
1 onion, minced
½ quart (approximately 500 ml) unshucked
  mussels
Parsley
2 tablespoons (30 ml) lard
2 tomatoes, chopped
Salt and pepper

Brown the rice in the oil with the minced onion.

Carefully clean the mussels and place in a sauce-pan with the parsley and lard in a hot oven (450°F, 220°C) until the shells open. When they have opened, remove the shells and carefully collect the liquid.

Add the mussels and the tomatoes to the rice.

Season with salt and pepper and moisten with the reserved liquid. Turn into a casserole and bake the whole mixture 25-30 minutes in a 350°F (180°C) oven.

Do not be awed by the task of cleaning mussels. Simply arm yourself with a sharp knife for the removal of appending beards and seaweed, and a plastic scourer for giving the shells a good scrub and quantities of cold water.

Cod Provençale

Garlic was handed out to the Roman soldiers to aid their courage — but spurned by the aristocracy as vulgar.

5 potatoes
4 tablespoons (60 ml) butter
2 skinless cod fillets, cooked and flaked
1 clove of garlic, finely chopped
Parsley, chopped

Cook potatoes in salted, boiling water. Drain and remove skins, dice and sauté in butter until golden.

Before the potatoes have browned completely, add the 2 cod fillets and chopped garlic and parsley. Serve piping hot.

Grilled Smelts

The skin lifts off smelts prepared this way in a single piece. The flesh is very tender.

30 fresh smelts
2 tablespoons (30 ml) coarse salt
Juice from 1 lemon
Pepper
3 tablespoons (45 ml) melted butter

Sprinkle the smelts with salt and let stand 30 minutes.

Drain them and suspend each for a moment by the tail to get rid of excess salt.

Pre-heat the broiler. Arrange the smelts in a pan and broil them 5 minutes or so on each side.

Combine the lemon juice, pepper and melted butter, pour over the smelts. Serve immediately.

Scallop Soufflé

¾ pound (approximately 350 g) scallops
2 tablespoons (30 ml) butter
2 tablespoons (30 ml) flour
1 cup (250 ml) milk
3 eggs, separated
6 tablespoons (90 ml) grated gruyère cheese
Parsley, finely chopped
Salt and pepper

Poach the scallops 15 minutes in a little water or court-bouillon. Drain and cut them in quarters.

In a small saucepan, heat the butter, stir in the flour, and add the milk, stirring constantly to make a smooth sauce.

Add the 3 egg yolks, the scallops, cheese, parsley and salt and pepper. Let cool.

Fold in the egg whites beaten to stiff peaks.

Prepare a 1½ quart (1.5*l*) soufflé dish with a buttered paper collar. Pour in the mixture and bake 30 minutes in a 350°F (180°C) oven. Serve while puffed and hot.

Fish Fillets on Toast

4 onions
1 tablespoon (15 ml) oil
3 tablespoons (45 ml) butter
4 fish fillets, any kind
Salt and pepper
1 cup (250 ml) dry white wine, or water
4 slices of bread
Cooking oil to fry the bread in

Mince the onions and sauté in the oil and butter just until they change color. Add the fish and salt and pepper and brown until golden.

Add the wine or water and simmer 20 minutes, covered.

Meanwhile, fry the bread slices in oil. Let drain on absorbent paper. Place the fish on the fried bread. Keep warm.

Reduce the sauce in half by boiling it uncovered, and pour over each serving.

Pâtés

All recipes serve four

Cognac and Sherry Pâté

½ pound (approximately 250 g) bacon slices
1 pound (approximately 500 g) minced beef
1 pound (approximately 500 g) minced pork
2 crushed cloves of garlic
4 tablespoons (60 ml) chopped parsley
½ teaspoon (2 ml) tarragon
½ teaspoon (2 ml) thyme
Pepper
1½ teaspoons (7 ml) salt
½ teaspoon (2 ml) paprika
2 eggs, beaten
4 ounces (100 ml) Cognac
1 pound (approximately 500 g) minced ham
1½ teaspoons (7 ml) dry mustard
1½ teaspoons (7 ml) nutmeg
4 ounces (100 ml) dry sherry
1 cup (250 ml) chopped shallots
½ cup (125 ml) chopped parsley
1 cup (250 ml) chopped onions

"Cooking is like love. It should be entered into with abandon or not at all"—
Harriet van Horne, Vogue, October 15, 1956.

Line a rectangular mold with some strips of bacon.

Mix together the beef, pork, garlic, 4 tablespoons parsley (60 ml), tarragon, thyme, pepper, salt, paprika, eggs and Cognac. In a second bowl, mix the ham, mustard, nutmeg, sherry and shallots. In a third bowl, mix ½ cup (125 ml) parsley and onions.

Spread ¼ of the beef mixture in the mold. Then add ½ cup (125 ml) of raw onions and chopped parsley. Then add half the ham mixture and sprinkle on the remaining onions and parsley. Add half the beef mixture followed by the second half of the ham mixture. Top with a layer of beef.

Cover with remaining bacon. Put foil over the top and bake 3-3½ hours in a 325°F (170°C) oven. Remove from the oven. Lift off the foil and press the pâté to remove the excess juice. Cool.

Hard-Cooked Egg Pâté

2 slices of bread with the crusts removed
¼ cup (50 ml) milk
2 tablespoons (30 ml) butter
2 tablespoons (30 ml) flour
1 cup (250 ml) scalded milk (see page 56)
¾ pound (approximately 350 g) minced beef
¼ pound (approximately 125 g) sausage meat
1 egg, raw
Parsley, chopped
Salt and pepper
Pinch of dry mustard
4 ounces (100 ml) Cognac
2 eggs, hard-cooked and shelled

Soak the bread in the ¼ cup (50 ml) of milk.

Melt the butter in a double boiler. Add the flour, stir and cook a few minutes. Slowly add the scalded milk and stir just until the sauce is thickened. Let cool, then cover and chill.

Combine in a bowl the minced beef, sausage meat, raw egg, parsley and soaked bread. Beat with a spoon for at least 10 minutes. Add the salt, pepper, and mustard, then the Cognac and cream sauce. Stir thoroughly.

On a piece of aluminum foil, arrange the mixture to form a square 1½ inches (3 cm) thick. (You will be making up the pâté as if it were a jelly roll.)

Place the eggs on the meat mixture in a line end to end on the exact center. Using the sheet of foil, seal the meat mixture over the eggs rolling the mixture on itself. Close the outer edges of the foil.

Place in a buttered pan and bake in a 350°F (180°C) oven for at least 40 minutes. Remove the aluminum foil after cooling overnight.

Place on a serving plate and garnish with slices of lemon, tomatoes and whole pickles.

Calves Liver Pâté

1 pound (approximately 500 g) calves liver
½ pound (approximately 250 g) sausages or
    sausage meat
1 teaspoon (5 ml) salt
½ teaspoon (2 ml) pepper
4 tablespoons (60 ml) parsley, chopped fine
1 cup (250 ml) celery, chopped
2 onions, chopped fine
¼ teaspoon (1 ml) thyme
¼ teaspoon (1 ml) cloves
1 egg, beaten
6 slices bacon
4 ounces (100 ml) Cognac

Black pepper has been valued since the Middle Ages when it was tender for dowries and taxes. The varieties range in flavor from the pungent "Lampong" to the mild "Sarawak". "Tellicherry" from the Northern Malabar coast is traditionally the most expensive.

Chop the liver and blend in a blender.

If you use sausages, remove the skin and take them apart. Add the sausage meat and the other ingredients to the liver. Mix together well.

Lay the slices of bacon in the bottom of a buttered oven-proof dish, and cover with the sausage and liver mixture.

Bake 1½ hours in a 300°F (150°C) oven.

When you take the pâté from the oven, sprinkle with Cognac and chill overnight.

Variation: Port can be substituted for the Cognac.

Rabbit Pâté

1 rabbit, 4 pounds (approximately 2 kg)
½ pound (approximately 250 g) pork
½ pound (approximately 250 g) veal
¼ pound (approximately 125 g) fat bacon
¼ pound (approximately 125 g) lean bacon
1 bottle dry white wine
Salt and pepper
½ teaspoon (2 ml) allspice
¼ teaspoon (1 ml) thyme
Bay leaf
1 ounce (25 ml) brandy or Calvados

Skin and draw the rabbit and cut evenly into pieces. Cut the pork, veal and bacon into thin strips. Add the white wine, salt, pepper, spices, thyme and bay leaf. Cover and marinate for 24 hours. Stir from time to time.

Turn into a large kettle, add the brandy and cook 2 hours over slow heat until the rabbit meat comes away from the bones. If necessary, add a little hot water.

Lift the pieces of meat from the sauce and arrange in an earthenware dish, alternating the meats.

Sieve the cooking juices and pour over the meat. Let cool then cover with waxed paper and a plate with a weight on top. Chill.

After 24 hours, unmold and serve on lettuce with gherkins.

Pork Rillettes

2½ pounds (approximately 1200 g) pork shoulder, cubed
2 teaspoons (10 ml) salt
1 teaspoon (5 ml) pepper
½ onion, chopped
¾ cup (175 ml) chicken stock
1½ teaspoons (7 ml) lemon juice
¾ cup (175 ml) dry white wine
4 cloves of garlic, peeled

Place all ingredients except the garlic in a pot with a good lid. Stew for 1½ hours. Add the cloves of garlic one minute before the end of the cooking time.

Remove from heat and beat steadily with electric mixer for approximately 10 minutes until the meat is well-minced and the mixture has cooled down.

Turn into a small stone crock and refrigerate overnight.

To those unfamiliar with garlic a little seems like a lot, but as you become more accustomed to it you will have to increase the quantities in order to obtain the desired strength of flavor — or add an extra squeeze of garlic juice at the end of the cooking time.

Liver Pâté

1½ pounds (approximately 725 g) chicken livers
½ pound (approximately 250 g) pork fat
1 small onion, finely chopped
1 stalk of celery, finely chopped
1 sprig of parsley, finely chopped
½ cup (approximately 125 ml) mushrooms,
    finely chopped
¼ green pepper, finely chopped
2 tablespoons (30 ml) butter
2 eggs
¼ teaspoon (1 ml) nutmeg
¼ teaspoon (1 ml) cinnamon
¼ teaspoon (1 ml) powdered cloves
1 teaspoon (5 ml) each of salt and pepper
Bacon slices, thin
1 bay leaf

Soak the chicken livers 20 minutes in salted water.
Dry thoroughly and put through a mincer with the
pork fat.

Brown the chopped vegetables in butter. Blend
with the chicken liver mixture. Put through the
mincer again, and sieve.

Add the eggs, one at a time, beating thoroughly
after each addition. Add the nutmeg, cinnamon,
cloves, salt and pepper.

Line a rectangular mold with thin slices of
bacon. Fill with the pâté mixture. Cover with
bacon slices. Place the bay leaf on the top. Bake
2½ hours in a 300°F (150°C) oven. Cool.

Vegetables

All recipes serve four

Mushrooms with Noodles

¼ pound (approximately 125 g) mushrooms,
   finely chopped
¼ pound (approximately 125 g) onions,
   finely chopped
2 tablespoons (30 ml) butter
4 tablespoons (60 ml) tomato paste
½ pound (approximately 250 g) noodles
Salt and pepper
2 tablespoons (30 ml) butter

A mycologist is a connoisseur of mushrooms. Take one with you on country rambles in the fall.

Brown the mushrooms and onions in butter and add the tomato paste.

Cook the noodles according to the directions on the package in a large quantity of salted boiling water. Drain.

Arrange half the noodles in a buttered baking dish, cover with the mushroom mixture and top with the remaining noodles.

Season with salt and pepper and sprinkle with melted butter.

Bake 30 minutes in a 350°F (180°C) oven.

Potato Pancake

5 potatoes
2 eggs, beaten
Salt and pepper
¼ pound (approximately 125 g) butter

Cook the potatoes in the water with their skins on. Peel, mash and blend in the beaten eggs. Add the salt and pepper.

Melt the butter in a frying pan and set half aside. Turn the mixture into the pan with half the butter and brown on one side. Add the rest of the butter before browning the other side. Serve hot.

Scalloped Potatoes

2 pounds (approximately 1 kg) potatoes
Milk
Cream
Salt
White pepper
2 tablespoons (30 ml) butter

Peel firm-fleshed potatoes and cut in paper thin slices.

Place in layers in a buttered dish, seasoning each layer with salt and pepper to taste. The level of potatoes should not come higher than ¾ the depth of the dish.

Cover the potatoes with milk mixed with fresh cream and dot the surface with little pieces of butter.

Bake at 300°F (150°C) for the first 20 minutes, then increase the heat to 325°F (170°C) for 30 - 35 minutes or until the potatoes are tender and the liquid is absorbed. The milk should scarcely boil.

White pepper is recommended mainly for aesthetic reasons when you wish to avoid the dark specks in light meat and fish dishes and sauces. White peppercorns are the fully ripened berries. The outer husk is rubbed off and only the inner part is dried in the sun.

Kidney Beans in Red Wine

½ pound (approximately 250 g) dried kidney
    beans
2 onions, whole
1 clove
½ lb. (approximately 250 g) salt pork
or
½ pound slab of bacon (approximately 250 g)
Salt
1 cup (250 ml) red wine
1 tablespoon (15 ml) butter
1½ tablespoons (20 ml) flour
3 sprigs of parsley

Soak the beans in cold water overnight. Cook
them in cold water to cover, adding the whole
onions, one stuck with a clove, and the bacon slab
or salt pork. Add salt when the water reaches the
boiling point. Heat the red wine and add to the
pot.

After 1½ hours of simmering covered over low
heat, remove the bacon or salt pork and cut it in
pieces. Return the pieces to the pot.

In a frying pan, melt the butter and stir in the
flour, letting it cook a few minutes. Add a little of
the bean broth to this to make a sauce and return
to the pot of beans.

Bring to the boil two or three times to thicken
the sauce and serve with a sprinkling of chopped
parsley.

Stuffed Tomatoes

8 tomatoes
2 tablespoons (30 ml) oil
5 slices of bread with the crusts removed
½ cup (125 ml) milk
½ pound (approximately 250 g) chopped, leftover
    meat (beef, pork, lamb or veal)
Salt and pepper
½ teaspoon (2 ml) Cayenne pepper
1 clove of garlic, crushed
1 tablespoon (15 ml) flour

To remove a tomato skin, first plunge the tomato into boiling water for 30 seconds, then into cold water. The skin slips off effortlessly.

Wash the tomatoes, wipe, and cut off the tops, scoop out the pulp and seeds.

Use the oil to grease a baking dish and place the tomato shells in it.

Prepare a stuffing with the bread soaked in milk and then drained, the tomato pulp, mashed, the chopped leftover meat, salt, pepper, Cayenne pepper and crushed garlic. Bind with the flour.

Fill the tomatoes with the stuffing and replace the tops. Bake 20 minutes in a 400°F (200°C) oven.

Eggplant with Butterfly Noodles

John Gerrard in his "Herbal" of 1597 warned his fellow Englishmen about the eggplant "...doubtless these apples have a mischievous quality, the use whereof is utterly to be forsaken". But we know better.

3 medium-sized tomatoes
½ pound (approximately 250 g) eggplant (1 medium-sized)
4 tablespoons (60 ml) oil
Salt and pepper
1 tablespoon (15 ml) parsley, finely chopped
½ pound (approximately 250 g) butterfly noodles
4 - 6 tablespoons (50 ml) grated gruyère cheese

Peel, seed, and cube the tomatoes, peel and cube the eggplant, and brown together in oil.

Reduce heat and simmer over low heat for 1 hour, and then season with salt and pepper. At the end of the cooking time, add the chopped parsley.

Cook the butterfly noodles in about 4 cups (1 *l*) salted boiling water. Drain and add to the tomato and eggplant mixture. Add the grated cheese and mix well.

A crushed clove of garlic may be added.

Salads

All recipes serve four

Grated Carrots with Cream

½ pound (approximately 250 g) carrots, raw
4 tablespoons (60 ml) fresh cream (35%)
Juice of a lemon
Salt

Scrub the carrots and grate them directly onto a serving platter. Sprinkle with cream, lemon juice, and salt.

The dish can be garnished with chopped parsley.

Belgian Endive with Beets

½ pound (approximately 250 g) Belgian endive
Vinaigrette dressing (see page 124)
¼ pound (approximately 125 g) cooked beets
   (Canned beets can be used or fresh beets cooked
   in salted water, skinned, cut in pieces and
   chilled.)

Wash the endive, wipe dry and tear into 1 inch (2.5 cm) pieces. Place in a bowl and sprinkle with vinaigrette dressing. Toss well. Leave in the dressing for about 20 minutes, tossing from time to time. Just before serving, garnish with cubed or sliced beets.

Green Bean Salad

1 pound (approximately 500 g) fresh green beans
½ pound (approximately 250 g) potatoes
¼ pound (approximately 125 g) lean bacon
2 tablespoons (30 ml) cider or wine vinegar
Pepper

Cook the beans and the potatoes separately, in salted, boiling water until just tender. Drain and let dry and cool.

Peel the potatoes and cut in slices and place in a bowl with the beans.

Dice the bacon and brown in a frying pan. Stir in the vinegar and pepper to make a warm sauce. Pour over the salad, toss and serve.

Canned green beans may be used, but they should be rinsed and then plunged for a few minutes into salted, boiling water and then drained to improve taste.

Green Peppers Meridional

4 green peppers
2 cloves of garlic peeled and quartered
½ cup (125 ml) olive oil

Stem the peppers. Grill them lightly so the outer skin can be scraped off gently.

Scoop out the peppers, cut them into thin strips, and place in a dish with the garlic between the layers. Cover with olive oil. Marinate for at least 24 hours.

Just before serving, remove the garlic. Serve very cold.

Dandelion Salad

½ pound (approximately 250 g) dandelion greens
4 eggs, hard-cooked
Vinaigrette dressing (see page 124)

Cut away the tough parts of the dandelion greens, and wash thoroughly in water. Drain dry and place in a bowl. Sprinkle with vinaigrette dressing.

Cut the hard-cooked eggs in quarters lengthwise. Arrange on the leaves.

This dish should be made only in the spring when the dandelion greens are tender.

Garlic is obviously an essential item in the medicine cabinet as a stomachic, antiseptic, cure for asthma, bronchitis and coughs, epilepsy, rheumatism, leprosy and the common cold — not to mention its value as an insect repellent.

Rainbow Salad

2 tablespoons (30 ml) minced ham
1 tin of mixed vegetables
2 tablespoons (30 ml) minced raw mushrooms
1 tart pickle
1 egg, hard-cooked
Olives, both green and black
A few leaves of lettuce, shredded
Mayonnaise (see page 124)

Toss together the ham, the vegetables, and the hard-cooked egg cut in slices. Arrange in a bowl and add mayonnaise. Mix well.

To improve the taste of the tinned vegetables, put them in a sieve and pour salted, boiling water over them.

Variation: Tinned or fresh cooked beets may be substituted for the tin of mixed vegetables.

Desserts

All recipes serve four

Pineapple Chantilly

1 fresh pineapple
¾ cup (175 ml) white sugar
¾ cup (175 ml) fresh cream (35%)
1 tablespoon (15 ml) butter
Fresh strawberries may be added.

Chantilly denotes a dish including quantities of fresh whipped cream, sweetened and flavored with vanilla or almond extract or liqueurs; and one which is sinfully calorific!

Cut the top off the pineapple, saving the top and the leaves. Remove the flesh and cut in small pieces. Put the hollowed out pineapple in the refrigerator.

Blend the sugar and ¾ of the pulp in the blender.

Whip the cream and fold into the blended mixture. Add the remaining pineapple cubes and fill the pineapple shell with this mixture.

Replace the top of the pineapple, using a little butter to help keep it on.

Refrigerate. Serve very cold.

Apricot Barquettes

2 heaping tablespoons (30 ml) butter, soft
½ cup (125 ml) sifted all-purpose flour
4 tablespoons (60 ml) white sugar
1 egg
Apricot jam
3 tablespoons (45 ml) powdered sugar

Cut the butter into little pieces and mix with the flour and the sugar.

Make a well in the center and add the egg. Blend lightly with a wooden spoon.

Knead the dough several times with the palm of the hand. Form into a ball and set aside for 1 hour, then roll out.

Butter individual barquette molds or any small boat-shaped molds and line with rolled out pastry. Bake 20 minutes in a 350°F (180°C) oven.

Allow to cool, and remove from the molds. Fill with apricot jam.

Sprinkle with powdered sugar and moisten with a little water. Glaze in a 400°F (200°C) oven for 2 minutes. Cool on a rack.

Apple Beignets (Fritters)

½ cup (125 ml) sifted all-purpose flour
1 egg, separated
1 teaspoon (5 ml) oil
1 teaspoon (5 ml) baking powder
Warm water
4 apples
Sugar to taste
Oil for deep frying

"I have never been able to sacrifice my appetite on the altar of my appearance" —
Robert Morley.

Put the flour in a bowl. Make a well in the center and add the yolk of the egg, the oil, and the baking powder and stir gently. Thin with warm water. Beat the egg whites with a fork for one minute and add to the mixture. Let stand 1 hour.

Scrub the apples, core, cut in rings, pat dry and dip in the frying batter.

Drop into hot deep fat, remove and drain when golden. Sprinkle with sugar to taste. Serve hot.

Other fruits may be substituted for the apples: apricots, bananas, etc.

Tropical Cream

4 egg yolks
¾ cup (175 ml) white sugar
1½ cups (375 ml) scalded milk (see page 56)
1 small tin crushed pineapple, drained
4 ounces (100 ml) kirsch

Beat the egg yolks in a bowl, with a spoon.

Add, bit by bit, the scalded milk, to which the sugar has been added.

Heat this mixture in the top of a double boiler stirring constantly. Blend in the pineapple.

Just before the custard is set, add the kirsch.

Chill.

Variation: The kirsch may be replaced by rum.

Cherries Meringuées

1 pound (500 g) sweet cherries
½ cup (125 ml) white sugar
2 egg whites

Cut the stems off the cherries to within ½ inch (1 cm) of the fruit. Wash and wipe dry.

Beat the egg whites 5 minutes with a fork. Dip the cherries in the egg then in sugar.

Arrange on a baking sheet powdered with sugar and bake 15 minutes in a 300°F (150°C) oven. Serve hot, warm or cold.

Coeur à la Crème

1 8-ounce package (approximately 250 g)
   cream cheese
7 tablespoons (100 ml) sugar
2 tablespoons (30 ml) fresh cream (35%)
½ cup (125 ml) milk
4 tablespoons (60 ml) apricot jam or raspberry
   or strawberry jam
or
4 ounces (125 g) fresh raspberries

Beat the cream cheese with the sugar, the cream and the milk until smooth.

Add the jam or fresh fruit. Blend.

Chill and serve in individual dessert dishes. Or place ingredients in the traditional heart-shaped coeur à la crème wicker basket lined with moistened cheesecloth. Chill, unmold and garnish with fresh fruit.

Apple and Pear Upside Down Cake

Most pears should be picked from the tree before they are fully ripe. They become sweet and juicy in the fruit bowl.

½ cup (125 ml) sifted all-purpose flour
3 eggs
1 generous cup (250 ml) milk
1 heaping tablespoon (15 ml) butter
1 pinch of salt
2 teaspoons (10 ml) rum
1 pound (approximately 500 g) apples and pears, very finely chopped

To make batter put the flour in a bowl, make a well in the center and break the eggs into it. Blend.

Scald the milk (see page 56), remove from the heat, and add the butter.

Pour the milk and butter mixture slowly into the egg and flour mixture, stirring with a wooden spoon.

Add the salt and rum and blend well. Arrange the finely chopped apples and pears in a buttered baking dish. Pour the batter over them and cook 10 minutes on the top of the stove over very low heat. Then bake 45 minutes in a 300°F (150°C) oven. Serve warm.

Fruit in Kirsch

1 apple
1 pear
20 sweet cherries
1 peach
20 grapes, green or red
¼ pound (approximately 125 g) raspberries
½ cup (125 ml) sugar
2 ounces (50 ml) kirsch

It's easier to whip cream if you place the bowl and beaters in the refrigerator about an hour before you begin.

Arrange the fruit in a bowl, cutting the larger fruits into slices or pieces. Sprinkle with sugar and kirsch. Serve cold.

Variation: Rum may be used in place of kirsch and the dish may be garnished with whipped cream.

Compote of Dried Fruits

½ pound (approximately 250 g) dried prunes
½ pound (approximately 250 g) dried figs
½ pound (approximately 250 g) raisins
½ cup (125 ml) white sugar
1 generous cup (250 ml) water
1 teaspoon (5 ml) vanilla
15 almonds
15 walnuts

Wash, drain, and soak the fruit in cold water for 2 hours. Simmer in the water with the sugar and vanilla over low heat for an hour. Turn into a serving dish, chill and garnish with the nuts.

Easy Raspberry Mousse

2 egg whites
4 tablespoons (60 ml) raspberry jam
Water

Beat the egg whites to stiff peaks. Thin the jam with a very little water, and blend gently with the egg whites. Serve immediately.

Variation: Strawberry jam may be substituted for raspberry.

Puffy Chocolate Omelette

¼ pound (125 g) unsweetened chocolate
¼ cup (50 ml) water
4 tablespoons (60 ml) white sugar
4 eggs, separated

Melt the chocolate in the water in the top of a double boiler.

Beat the sugar and egg yolks together until lemon colored. Add the melted chocolate little by little, beating well.

Beat the egg whites into stiff peaks, and fold them into the custard mixture.

Butter a rectangular cake tin, turn the mixture into it and bake 5 minutes in a 400°F (200°C) oven.

Remove from the oven and make 4 or 5 cuts in the top with a knife. Put back in the oven for 5 minutes to allow the insides to cook. Serve immediately.

Chocolate! Montezuma, a short-sighted Aztec ruler, consumed hot chocolate by the pitcher but forbade the women to touch it on the grounds that it was an aphrodisiac.

Pears with Vanilla Custard

4 medium-sized pears
5 tablespoons (75 ml) white sugar
1 tablespoon (15 ml) rum
1 teaspoon (5 ml) vanilla
3¾ cups (700 ml) milk
1 teaspoon (5 ml) vanilla
½ cup (125 ml) sugar
5 egg yolks
1 teaspoon (5 ml) cornstarch

Peel the pears, place in a saucepan and cover with water. Add sugar, rum and 1 teaspoon (5 ml) vanilla. Cover and let simmer 50 minutes.

Bring the milk to the boiling point. Add the rest of the vanilla.

In a bowl, mix the sugar, the egg yolks, and the cornstarch diluted in a little cold water.

Add the milk flavored with vanilla in a steady stream, stirring constantly. Turn into a saucepan and cook over low heat, stirring constantly until just thickened.

Let chill, stirring frequently.

Lift the pears out of the cooking juices and put in a serving dish, cover them with the vanilla custard. Chill.

Peaches in Rum

4 peaches
4 tablespoons (60 ml) butter
1 tablespoon (15 ml) white sugar
2 ounces (50 ml) water
2 tablespoons (30 ml) rum

Peel the peaches, cut them in two and put a mixture of butter and sugar where the pit was.

Arrange in an oven-proof dish, sprinkle with water and rum, and bake 40 minutes in a 350°F (180°C) oven. Serve hot.

Prunes in Red Wine

1 cup (250 ml) dry red wine
¼ teaspoon (1 ml) cinnamon
4 tablespoons (60 ml) sugar
½ pound (approximately 250 g) prunes

Bring to the boil the wine with the cinnamon and sugar and simmer until the sugar has dissolved.

Lower the prunes into the wine, return to the boil and take off the heat when the boiling point is reached again.

Turn into a fruit dish and let cool.

This dessert tastes even better when prepared 2 or 3 days in advance.

Any plum can become a prune provided that it can be dried successfully and keeps well when dried. They are often neglected but particularily valuable in the winter — rich in vitamins with well-known restorative powers.

Curaçao Soufflé

¼ pound (approximately 125 g) candied fruit
1 ounce (25 ml) curaçao
5 tablespoons (75 ml) flour
2 tablespoons (30 ml) butter
¾ cup (175 ml) milk, scalded (see page 56)
6 eggs, separated
5 tablespoons (75 ml) sugar
1 teaspoon (5 ml) vanilla

Cut up the candied fruit in small pieces and soak in the curaçao.

Scald the milk and add the sugar and vanilla.

Melt the butter in the top of a double boiler and blend in the flour. Cook for a few minutes.

Add the hot milk then the egg yolks one at a time, stirring steadily. Let cool.

Add the fruit and curaçao.

Beat the egg whites into stiff peaks. Fold them delicately into the mixture.

Half fill a soufflé dish with the mixture.

Bake 10 minutes at 350°F (180°C) then for 25 minutes at 450°F (230°C). Serve at once.

Basic recipes

Tomato Sauce

6 medium-sized tomatoes, peeled and sliced
1 tablespoon (15 ml) vegetable oil
Salt and pepper
1 clove of garlic or 1 onion, minced
Chopped parsley to taste

Put all the ingredients in a saucepan and simmer 15 minutes. To obtain a more velvety sauce you can blend the ingredients in a blender before cooking.

To fully appreciate the flavor of pepper only use it freshly-ground. Include it during the cooking period, but for the complete spicey aroma add a few extra grinds from the mill at the end.

Court-Bouillon

2 cups (500 ml) salted water
2 sprigs of parsley
1 onion
Salt and pepper
Thyme
Bay leaf
1 whole clove

Put all ingredients in a saucepan. Bring almost to the boil. Simmer 15 minutes. Let cool. Then add the fish you are cooking and let simmer.

Simple Mayonnaise

When making mayonnaise you will find that everything blends together better when the oil, eggs, bowl, etc. are at room temperature— and when the weather is not thundery or oppressive.

2 egg yolks
1 teaspoon (5 ml) Dijon-type mustard
1 cup (250 ml) olive oil
1 teaspoon (5 ml) cider or wine vinegar
Salt and pepper

Put the egg yolks and mustard in a deep bowl. Stir with a wooden spoon.

Add the oil drop by drop at the beginning. After it emulsifies, add the rest of the oil in a stream, and the vinegar. Stir.

Season to taste with salt and pepper.

Vinaigrette Dressing

Salt and pepper
1 teaspoon (5 ml) dry mustard
1 tablespoon (15 ml) cider vinegar
3 tablespoons (45 ml) olive oil

Put the salt, pepper and mustard in a bowl. Add the vinegar and blend well. Gradually beat in the oil.

Home-Style Ketchup

1 28-ounce tin (approximately 800 ml) tomatoes
  or fresh tomatoes peeled and thinly sliced
1 cup (250 ml) white vinegar
3 large onions, chopped
3 large apples, peeled, cored and cut in flakes
1 cup (250 ml) white sugar
Salt and pepper
1 tablespoon (15 ml) pickling spices

In a saucepan put the tomatoes, the vinegar, the onions and the apples. Add the sugar, salt and pepper and the pickling spices wrapped in cheesecloth.

Cook 1 hour over slow heat. Remove the spices at the last moment. Pour into sterilized jars. Makes a 32 ounce (approximately 1 *l*) jar.

Unfortunately there appears little evidence to support the claim that the tomato has aphrodisiacal powers. It seems a mere misunderstanding, a breakdown in communication . . . the tomato was called a "love-apple" translated from "pommes d'amour", a corruption of "pomi dei moro" (Spaniard's apple). The Spaniards had first come across them in South America.

Basic Pie Dough

1 2/3 cup (425 ml) sifted all-purpose flour
4 tablespoons (60 ml) butter
2 tablespoons (60 ml) oil
4 ounces (100 ml) cold water
A pinch of salt

Put the flour in a bowl.

In a saucepan, melt the butter and add the oil and water to it.

Add this mixture to the flour. Mix rapidly with a wooden spoon until the dough has an even consistency. Form the dough into a ball. Let rest 2 hours before using.

If you are making a pre-cooked pie shell, roll out the dough and line a pie plate. Line the pie shell with buttered tinfoil and place beans or stones in it to help retain the shape. Cook 16 minutes in a 400°F (200°C) oven. Remove, take out beans and tinfoil and return to the oven for a minute or two. Reduce the cooking time if the pie shell is to be partially cooked.

Index

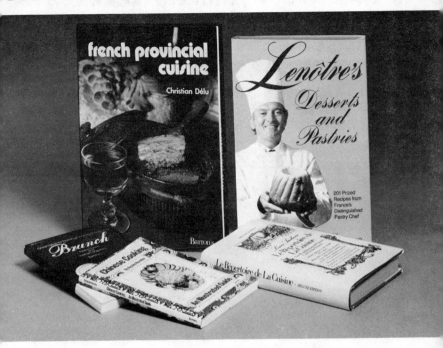

French Provincial Cuisine   Christian Délu, $15.95 cl.

A new cookbook with over 240 recipes, and 180 full-color photographs. Includes specialties of various regions with easy-to-follow recipes for appetizers, soups, vegetables, fish, meats, salads, and desserts.

Lenôtre's Desserts and Pastries

Lenôtre, France's famous pastry chef, $15.95 cl.
With step-by-step procedures for making puff pastries, meringues, eclairs, brioche, and many other delights.

Le Répertoire de La Cuisine   Louis Saulnier

$7.95 cloth, standard edition; $12.95 cloth, deluxe edition
The classic reference to French culinary terms used by restaurateurs for years. Explains the ingredients for all classic French dishes.

How to Recognize 30 Edible Mushrooms

Antoine Devignes, $4.95 pa.
A field guide that simplifies the process of identifying species. With color photos of each species, plus hints on locating and cooking.

Chinese Cooking   Ayako Namba, $3.95 pa.

Regional specialties, with suggestions on selecting and preparing the dishes, serving customs, proper utensils, and so forth.